The Family of Geo W & Malisa J Gunter

(An Oklahoma Pioneer Family)

Sharalyn Stewart

COVER PHOTO

Malisa Gunter (far right) with grandchildren standing in front of the original house built on the Gunter's Canute homestead.

(Photo contributed by George Gunter)

This composition is dedicated to my mother

Mary Ellen Stevens-Stewart

CONTENTS

Land that was the homestead's cotton field on Turkey Creek near Canute

ACKNOWLEDGMENTS

I would like to extend a special 'Thank You' to those who contributed information

Jeanne Gunter, daughter of Albert Gunter; **George Gunter**, son of John Gunter; **Janet Gunter**, daughter of John Gunter; **Stephen Brown**, grandson of Bessie Gunter; **Kendall Brown**, grandson of Bessie Gunter; **Ronald Lutes**, grandson of Rosa Gunter; **Lennel Davenport**, ex-daughter-in-law of Bessie Gunter; **Debbie Czernoch**, granddaughter of Rosa Gunter; **Anita Garvin**, granddaughter-in-law of Albert Gunter; **Glenn E Harlinger, Jr.,** grandson of Albert Gunter; **Jack Gunter**, son of John Gunter; **Betty Gunter**, daughter-in-law of Albert Gunter; **Ruby Menard**, daughter of Irene Gunter; **Nicky Barmettler**, granddaughter of Albert Gunter; **Itha Harrington**, granddaughter of Albert Gunter; **Tonya Gunter**, granddaughter of Albert Gunter, **Henry Stringer**, son of Irene Gunter, **Shawn Quilao**, granddaughter of Albert Gunter, **Harry Ammerman, Jr.,** grandson of Rosa Gunter, **Warren Char**, stepson of Jerry L Titus, **Brenda Wiers**, granddaughter of Rosa Gunter, **Vincent Geesman**, great-grandson of Albert Gunter

Photographs contributed from the following sources:

The Collection of Malisa Gunter, The Collection of Ollie Gunter-Stevens, The Collection of Mary Ellen Stevens-Stewart, The Collection of Vida Mae Gunter-Sanderson, The Collection of Janet Gunter, The Collection of George Gunter, The Collection of Robin Stewart-Dickerson, The Collection of Amber Stewart-Fankhauser, The Collection of Angela Stewart, The Collection of Debbie Czernoch, The Collection of Jack Gunter, The Collection of Nicky Gunter-Barmettler, The Collection of Tonya Gunter, The Collection of Shawn Harrington-Quilao, The Collection of Harry Ammerman, Jr., The Collection of Vincent Geesman,

INTRODUCTION

My mother, Mary Ellen Stevens-Stewart was proud of her heritage. Mom loved relaying stories told her by family members and memories she held of her childhood. The Gunter lineage was one branch on her ancestry tree she remained curious about, prompting her to read all information she could find available on the subject.

Hoping to fill in blanks regarding my great-grandparents and their descendants, the research has led to relatives I heard mom mention but never imagined contacting, much more meeting face to face. It has been a wonderful experience. My sincere thanks to each who have graciously taken time to assist with materials and information to make this project possible.

Informational content within the covers of this booklet has been gleaned from many sources: personal experience, stories told by my grandma and mom, documents saved by my great-grandmother, grandmother, and mother, licenses and certificates gathered through research, and relatives spoken with. Multiple sources found on the internet have also been tapped; ancestry.com, Find-A-Grave.com, familysearch.org, the Oklahoma Historical Society, Crawfordsville Public Library, and general Google searches.

My favorite hobbies are writing and doing research. This project has combined my two obsessions. It has been a wonderful outlet and a productive way to spend my time while sitting at the computer. The content is in no way professional. 'It is what it is' based on my capability. I apologize in advance for format errors, typographical mistakes, and any inaccuracies due to misinformation. I have cross-referenced and verified contents when possible.

Note: In editing I chose to leave out exact birth dates and specific location of birth for all living descendants. This decision was based in part to respecting privacy and partly due to security we must be conscious of in this day and time. For those who shared this information I am grateful but feel it best if specifics are left unpublished.

Lawson

William L Lawson (Dock) was born 6 Sep 1835 in Tennessee, the son of David and Elizabeth (Craig) Lawson. William's mother died when he was very young. Tennessee marriage records show his father David remarried in Jan 1839. When William moved his family to Texas, his father David moved the majority of his family as well, both settling in the Waco area.

David Lawson was born 14 Jan 1802 in Virginia. He was the youngest son of Sarah Lawson. His father is unknown. Tennessee Marriage Records show David Lawson married Elizabeth Craig on 20 Feb 1829 in Rhea County. She died prior to 1839. He married twice after the death of Elizabeth. David died on 14 Mar 1879 in McLennan County, Texas. He is buried at Bosqueville Cemetery in Bosqueville, McLennan County, Texas. (findagrave.com)

Sarah Lawson was born around 1776 in Virginia. She was the daughter of John Lawson. Her mother is unknown.

John Lawson was born about 1756 in Virginia. His parents are unknown.

Snyder/Snider/Schneider

Martha Caroline Snyder was born in 1837 in Blount County, Tennessee. She was the daughter of Moses and Phoebe (Roddy) Snyder. (ancestry.com)

Moses Snyder was born 4 Apr 1804 in Tuckaleechee Cove, Blount County, Tennessee and died 14 Apr 1886 in McMinn County, Tennessee. He was the son of Peter and Mary (Montgomery) Snider. Moses married Phoebe Roddy, born 3 Mar 1812 in Tennessee.[i] She died 17 Jun 1897 in McMinn County, Tennessee.[ii] Her parents are unknown.

Peter Snider was born 9 Jul 1776 in Dunmore, Shenandoah County, Virginia. He was the son of Johann Georg and Elizabeth Schneider. Peter married Mary Montgomery, born 16 Feb 1777 in North Carolina. She died 26 Mar 1870 in Blount County, Tennessee. Peter died 21 Feb 1867 in Tuckaleechee Cove, Blount County, Tennessee. [iii]

Johann Georg Schneider was born 1733 in Baden-Wuerttemberg, Germany. In 1752 he and two brothers immigrated to Pennsylvania. On 17 Dec 1765 he married Elizabeth last name unknown in Lancaster, Chester County, Pennsylvania. She was born about 1750. After marriage Johann with his wife migrated to Virginia, eventually settling in the Shenandoah area. He died 20 Oct 1785 in Shenandoah County, Virginia. Elizabeth died 10 Jun 1792 in Shenandoah County, Virginia. (ancestry.com)

Peter and Mary Snyder

The Union of Lawson/Snyder

William L Lawson married **Martha Caroline Snyder** on 4 Sep 1854 in McMinn County, Tennessee. (ancestry.com/Tennessee Marriage Records)

In the 1860 US Census William and Martha are living in Meigs County, Tennessee. William owns real estate valued at $1500.00 with personal property valued at $223.00.

A gap in children's births between 1862 to 1867 indicates it is likely William was a participant in the Civil War during this time span. By 1867 William and Martha are residing in Texas. It gives the impression William left Tennessee soon after the Confedercy fell to the Union. Both William and his father David sell their Tennessee lands and move their family to the Waco, Texas area.

In the 1870 Census taken on 28 Aug both William and his father are residing in McLennan County, Texas, west of the Brazos River. Value of William's personal property is listed as $200.00.

By 1880 the US Census shows William has left the Waco area, moving onto Hood County, Texas. Texas Marriage Records indicate they were living there when daughter Mary Elizabeth married David Reed Casey in Hood County, Texas on 21 Jun 1879. (ancestry.com/Texas Marriage Records)

It is unknown when William and Martha left Hood County, Texas to settle in Chickasaw Nation, Indian Territory (Oklahoma) near Homer, a small community north of Hennepin. There is record of William and Martha's daughter, Elizabeth Lawson Casey having a son, Tom Arthur Casey born Nov 1887 in Homer, Indian Territory (Oklahoma). It is likely William and Martha was also living there. In Indian Territory, for five dollars a settler could secure from the Indian Tribe a 5-year lease consisting of farm and pastureland, with stipulation improvements were made upon the homestead.

The 1900 US Census taken 23 Jun lists William and Martha living in Chickasaw Nation Indian Territory near Hennepin (Township 23 Range 2 W). William is a renter with occupation listed as farmer. The census states both William and Martha can read and write. Daughters Lizzie (who is a widow) and Texanna (who is single) are living with their parents, as are Lizzie's three children; Lizzie. Tom, and Emma. (ancestry.com)

In 1909 William passed away in Garvin County near Hennepin, Oklahoma. He is buried in Murray County in an unmarked grave at the Hennepin Cemetery located a few miles south of the Hennepin community.

After William's death Martha relocated to Graham in Carter County, Oklahoma. In the 1910 US Census Martha is listed as Emma C Lawson, head of household. Martha states she is widowed and has had twelve children with nine living. Residing in the home are daughters Phoebe C Casey (Elizabeth Casey) and Texanna Wright who are also widowed, and a grandson William W Wright.

In 1913 Martha passes away in Healdton, Carter County, Oklahoma. A story told in the Wright family was that on a brutal wintery day Martha was taken by wagon from Graham to Hennepin for burial next to her husband William. She is buried in an unmarked grave at the Hennepin Cemetery south of Hennepin in Murray County, Oklahoma.

William L & Martha Caroline Lawson

Malisa Jane Lawson

Malisa Jane Lawson was born near Waco in McLennan County, Texas on 6 Mar 1869. She was the daughter of William L. and Martha Caroline (Snyder) Lawson. Malisa was referred to Liss or Lissie.

It is unknown why Malisa was left from the 1870 US Census taken on the date 28 Aug 1870. In the 1880 US Census she is listed as Mary Lawson born about 1872 in Texas. William and Martha's daughter Mary was born in 1860 and had married David Reed Casey by 1880. There is a separate census record for Mary and David Casey for 1880.

Unfortunately the 1890 Census was destroyed by a fire so there is no concrete census record of Malisa existing until the 1900 US Census where she is found living in Washita County, Oklahoma Territory (Oklahoma) married to George W. Gunter. (ancestry.com)

Little is known about Malisa's life prior to marrying George. Granddaughter Mary Ellen Stevens-Stewart shared a story told by her grandmother. When Malisa was a young girl she loved racing her horse in competition against her brothers and neighboring boys. Her grandmother bragged that even riding sidesaddle she usually won the race.

Gunter

George Washington Gunter was born 23 Dec 1871 in Jacksboro, Jack County, Texas. He was the son of Zachariah William and Anna (Gage) Gunter. He passed away 15 May 1943 in Elk City, Beckham County, Oklahoma. George is buried at the Canute Cemetery in Canute, Washita County, Oklahoma.

Zachariah William Gunter known as Zack was born 1839 in Green County, Arkansas. He was the youngest child of George Washington and Elizabeth 'Betsy' (Hutchins) Gunter.

Zack married Anna Gage 29 Oct 1862 in Jack County, Texas. Anna was born about 1844 in Phillips County, Arkansas. She was the daughter of Calvin and Mary Ann (Fowler) Gage. Anna passed away during the year 1876 in Jacksboro, Jack County, Texas.

On ancestry.com is found a Texas Muster Roll Index Card for Zac Gunter of Jack County, Texas with enlistment date of 1 Feb 1864. Rank is given as Private. Commissioned Officers are H J Thompson and T F Roberts, Captain, Major Wm. Quayle, Commanding.

Zack married Sarah A Hancock on 25 Mar 1882 in Texas. (familysearch.org)

Zack passed away during Apr 1892 in Jacksboro, Jack County, Texas. (ancestry.com)

George Gunter was born about 1800. The precise date of his birth and location are unknown. Information relating to his parentage is also a mystery.

George married Elizabeth Hutchins known as Betsy in Hatley, Monroe County, Mississippi during the year 1825. She was born 19 Jul 1804 in Warren County, Georgia, daughter of Zachariah and Charity (Shepard) Hutchins. (ancestry.com) Betsy passed away 18 Nov 1875 in Savoy, Fannin County, Texas.

The 1830 US Census list George and Betsy living in Hardeman County, Tennessee. They are recorded as living near Zachariah Hutchins, Betsy's father. (ancestry.com)

The Arkansas Census shows George and Betsy living in Lawrence County, Arkansas by the year 1833. The 1840 US Census records them living in Green County, Arkansas. (ancestry.com)

In 1850 George dies of cholera while crossing the Mississippi River. Mary Ellen Stevens-Stewart said she had always been told he was buried on a bank of the Mississippi but had no idea as to where.

Zachariah Gunter w/ niece Miss Fowler

Elizabeth 'Betsy' Gunter's Headstone

George Washington Gunter

George Washington Gunter was born near Jacksboro in Jack County, Texas. [1] It was stated by his daughter Vida Mae Sanderson that in old records he was referred to as George Gunter, Jr. Reason for this could be that when George was young he lived near his older cousin George W. Gunter, son of Wiley Gunter, Sr.

George's mother Anna died when he was around the age of four. In the 1880 US Census taken the 16th day of June George is recorded as being 8 years old and his father is listed as a widower. Granddaughter Mary Ellen Stevens-Stewart was of the impression his mother was killed by Indians. Information has not been found to verify cause of death. His father Zack married Sarah A Hancock in 1882. Mary Ellen stated her grandfather George spoke of being raised by a stepmother that he expressed a dislike toward.

George grew up a farm/ranch near Jacksboro in Jack County, Texas. The 1940 US Census gives his highest level of education completed as the 5th Grade.

As a young man George worked as a cowboy assisting his Gunter cousins on cattle drives into Indian and Oklahoma Territories.

It is unknown when George moved into Chickasaw Nation Indian Territory (Oklahoma) but record is found of other family members living in the territory early as 1889.

---

[1] Contradicting the birthdate inscribed on Geo W. Gunter's headstone and the birth year 1869 printed in his funeral pamphlet, George appears born in the year 1871. In Feb. 1869 George's older sister Mary Ellen Gunter was born. On the 22nd day of July 1870 the Federal Census lists John being 7 months old. John Calvin Gunter, George's older brother was born 7 Jan 1870. In the 1870 Census George is not listed with the household of Zachariah Gunter.

In the 1880 Federal Census George is listed as 8 years old on the 16th day of Jun making his birth year 1871. In census records both Mary Ellen and John Calvin are listed as being older than brother George. The 1920 Federal Census lists George two years younger than his wife Malisa. The 1930 Federal Census also lists Malisa being older than George. In the 1940 Federal Census George is again listed as two years younger than his wife who was born on 6 Mar 1869.

George W and Malisa J Gunter

Granddaughter Mary Ellen was of the belief her Gunter grandparents met in Jacksboro, Jack County, Texas. Last known location of the Lawson family prior to settling in Indian Territory was Hood County, Texas. By wagon it was a major trek to Jacksboro, Texas and off the beaten path into Indian Territory where the Lawson's settled. US Census records indicate that Zack Gunter's children and a niece had relocated to Indian Territory prior to 1890 and settled near the area where the Lawson family had settled.

Mary Ellen Stevens-Stewart said her grandparents, George Washington Gunter and Malisa Jane Lawson were married in Hennepin, Indian Territory in 1891. Upon request for copy of the marriage record it was stated by the court clerk that all documents prior to 1905 were destroyed by a fire.

After George and Malisa (Liss) married they settled into farm life and began raising a family near the small pioneer settlement of Homer. Research indicates Homer was few miles north of Hennepin. The settlement no longer exists but Homer can be found on Oklahoma maps published in 1895 and 1905. It is believed this was the birth location of Ollie and Bessie, and possibly Rosie. Albert has stated on several documents that he was born near Ardmore.

Malisa's brother James 'Jim' Lawson married George's sister, Effie C Gunter. Jim and Effie typically lived nearby.

Around 1898 George and Liss packed up the family and the wagon, rounded up the livestock, and headed out across the prairie to relocate to a parcel of land in Washita County, Oklahoma Territory. Studying old Oklahoma maps, it is possible their migration route to Washita County was by traveling on the Ft. Sill Arbuckle Road that ran near Wild Horse Creek and the community of Homer. Taking this road, they could have followed it toward Ft. Sill Military Reservation and then veered north on the Great Western Cattle Trail. This trail would lead past the eastern edge of the homestead George and Liss settled upon. Their daughter Vida Mae Gunter-Sanderson wrote in a letter sent to a niece (copy forwarded by Henry Stringer) that the farm was located along the eastern boundary of a cattle trail and buffalo wallow impressions remained on the land.

Arriving in the prairie wilderness of Northwestern Oklahoma, the Gunter family watched the birth and rise of the town of Canute, located approximately two miles west of their homestead. In October 1898, the Canute school district became the first consolidated school district in Washita County. A post office was established for the area on February 24, 1899. Also that year a general merchandise store was opened in what would later become the town site for Canute. In 1902 a railroad built tracks through the area. It is written that by then Canute already had a bank, cotton gin, and general merchandise store. By 1904 the town had two newspapers, two hotels, three doctors, a buggy works, a carpenter shop, a lumberyard, two cotton gins, two hardware and implement dealers, two livery stables, a drugstore, two saloons, a blacksmith shop, three general merchandise and grocery stores, two furniture stores with funeral supplies, and a music store as well as several attorneys, real estate businesses, two banks, a photographer, and an auctioneer.[iv] In 1918 the Canute jail was built.[v]

On the homestead near Turkey Creek everyone in the family worked hard to prove up the land for ownership. Liss and children worked the cotton field plantin', hoein', choppin', and pickin' cotton. Mary Ellen Stevens-Stewart once remarked her grandmother commented she worked in the cotton field until hours nearing the birth of a baby.

From a copy of the case file referencing George Gunter's land claim and application for homestead obtained from the National Archives for Land Records in Washington D.C. is the following information:

> On 10 Mar 1898 George Gunter of Burns applied for a homestead application at the Land Office at Oklahoma City, O.T. for the NW ¼ of Section 20 in Township 11 north of Range 19 west, I.M. containing 160 acres. Due to an error of the property description, this claim was amended on 8 Jul 1898 to read the SW ¼ of Section 17, Township 11 N, Range 19 W. The claim's Application Number remained 13233.

> An Affidavit of Notice of Publication was filed 18 Jul 1904 by G.L. Winn, Editor of the Canute Banner swearing notice of final proof by George Gunter of Canute, for Homestead. Number 13233 being the SW ¼ of Sec. 17 Twp 11 n Range 19 w I.M (Indian-Meridan) stating it was published in the Jun 10th, Jun 17th, Jun 24th, Jul 1st, Jul 8th, and Jul 15th editions of the Canute Banner in 1904.

> A certificate for posting of notice in the United States Land Office at El Reno, Oklahoma states a printed copy was posted in a conspicuous place in the office for a period of thirty days, having first posted said notice on 7 Jun 1904.

> On the document Homestead Proof—Testimony of Witness dated 18 Jul 1904, David L Simmons served as a witness in support of George's homestead entry for SW ¼, Twp 11 N Range 19 W of I. M. The testimony states the land is used for prairie and farming with 50 acres in cultivation. It reads George Gunter established residence on the property 1 Dec 1898. Improvements since that date included a house, a dugout, a well, an orchard, a corncrib, a corral, and a hen house. The land was all fenced and cross-fenced with 2 to 4 wire fences with post 30 feet apart. Total value, $700.00.

> The Final Certificate Number was 1740 for Homestead Application No. 13233, Oklahoma Series. Filed at the El Reno, Oklahoma land office 19 Jul 1904. The application was approved on 5 Feb 1905 and patented 3 Apr 1905, Recorded in Volume 160, page 10.

From an early age the Gunter children labored to keep abreast of household chores entailing the tasks of preparing daily meals, drawing water from the well, collecting prairie chips for the cook stove, churning butter, cleaning house, raising a garden, harvesting and preserving fruits from the family orchard, washing, drying, ironing, and mending laundry, sewing clothing and making quilts. The barnyard required their attention as well. There were cows to milk, hogs to slop, chickens and other barnyard fowl to feed and eggs to gather, horses and mules to tend, among a multitude of other daily responsibilities.

In the 1900 US Federal Census taken on 2 Jul, George is residing in Washita County in an area recorded as Elk-No.11. Living with him are his wife Malisa and children Albert, Rosa, Ollie and Bessie. The census states George and Malisa have been married nine years. Malisa is the mother of four children, with four children living. George states he is a farmer, owns his property, and he can read, write, and speak English but his wife cannot read or write.

In a photocopy of a letter received from Henry Stringer penned by Vida Gunter-Sanderson she writes, "The first few years were spent living in a dugout…The nearest town was El Reno ninety miles east and George made a trip there by wagon twice a year for supplies. Food staples were bought by the barrel and fabric by the bolt. By 1901 lumber was available and neighbors helped each other build houses, as well as harvest crops, make sorghum molasses, deliver babies, nurse the sick, and butcher meat."

In the 1910 Federal Census taken on the 3rd day of May George is recorded living in Turkey Creek Township in Washita County. Family members include wife Malisa, daughters Rosa, Ollie, Bessie, Betty, Hattie and Nellie, and son Lester (John). Malisa is the mother of eight children, all of which are living. George continues to farm as an occupation.

Continuing with information from the copied letter from Henry Stringer Vida wrote, "Drought years presented a problem as there was no stream of water on the farm. In 1915 he (George) and Albert had to drive the cattle to the mountains of New Mexico for grass and water. The drought continued for several years and George rented a ranch in Roger Mills County, one mile north of Herring. This was 30 miles from the farm and the trips back and forth were made by wagon until a Model-T Ford was purchased."

Vida included in the letter that in 1918 the entire family was affected by the flu pandemic sweeping across the nation, stating they all came down with and survived the Spanish Influenza and Small Pox epidemic.

In the 1920 Federal Census George is listed as living in East Turkey Creek, Washita County, Oklahoma with wife Malisa, and daughters Ollie, Bessie, Betty, Hattie, Nellie and Vida Mae. Betty, Hattie and Nellie are attending school.

In her letter Vida listed highlights the family enjoyed. Entertainment included attending the annual Fourth of July celebration and picnic held in Foss, the Beckham County Fair, and the Barnum and Bailey Circus when it visited Elk City. Sundays on the Gunter farm were often spent with neighboring children playing baseball and riding bucking calves.

Vida stated that in 1924 her father George purchased a portion of the John Gage ranch. The property was located nine miles north of Canute. George thereafter divided his time between the ranch and the farm.

The 1930 Federal Census indicates George and Malisa along with son John are living with son Albert and his family. On 7 Apr 1930 Albert states he is renting the farm in Turkey Creek Township and works as a farmer. The census states Malisa was 21 at time of first marriage and George was 20 years old. Neither Albert nor George are a war veteran.

In the mid-1930s son John Gunter and his family operated the Canute farm and George and Liss moved to the ranch in Custer County. During this time their son Albert's children came to the ranch to live with their Gunter grandparents.

In the 1940 Federal Census taken on 2 April George, Malisa and granddaughter Philathia are residing in Custer County, Range 20, Washita Twp. George owns his home valued at $300.00 and lists occupation as farmer, stating he worked approximately 30 weeks in 1939. For his residence in 1935 he gives the same location.

George passed away 15 May 1943 in Elk City, Beckham County, Oklahoma.

Taken from Mary Ellen Stevens-Stewart's collection of funeral cards, George's memorial pamphlet states: *George Washington Gunter was born 23 Dec 1868 and passed away 15 May 1943. Services were held at the Methodist Church in Canute, Oklahoma, officiated by Reverend Horace L. Janes with interment at Canute Cemetery.*

A legal document belonging to Malisa Gunter regarding her husband's estate reads as follows:

General Inventory & Appraisement
In County Court, County of Custer,
In the Matter of the Estate, G.W. Gunter, deceased,
No. 2814-P filed in 1943 by Malisa Gunter, Executor.

General Inventory and Appraisement
Estate of G W Gunter, deceased

Lists inventory of all Real Estate in Custer and Washita County Oklahoma and all (goods, chattels, rights, credits, and Estate of _____ deceased, except the homestead, which have come to my possession or knowledge

Real Estate:

NW ¼ and W ½ E ½ Section 3; and NW ¼ and W ½ NE ¼ Section 2; all in Twp 12 North Range 20, W.I. M. Custer County, Oklahoma.

SW ¼ Section 17, Twp 11, Range 19, W.I.M. Washita County, Oklahoma

Personal Property:

Money in First State Bank, Foss, Money in First State Bank, Canute, Cows, Cattle, Mares, Horses, Mules, and Hogs.

Following her husband's death Liss returned to the original homestead site near Canute. She lived in a small house located on the property while son John and family lived in the 'big house'. She remained on the farm until 1949 and then moved to Oklahoma City where she lived with daughter Ollie and son-in-law Dan Stevens.

The 1954 US City Directory published for Oklahoma City, Oklahoma, it lists Mrs. Melissa Gunter as residing at 3712 W Park Place.

In 1957 Malisa and her widowed daughter Ollie move to a newly built home near a rural community known as Midlothian in Lincoln County, Oklahoma. After relocation to the sandstone hillside Malisa spent her days relaxing in her rocker, often teaching great-granddaughter Sharalyn Stewart how to recite the alphabet and count to one-hundred prior to starting grade school.

On occasion Liss was known to take a small tin of Garret snuff from her apron pocket and snort a pinch. A larger glass container of the same brand tobacco was kept in her dresser drawer for refilling the small snuff can. When empty the glass container was cleaned and used as a juice glass or for giving great-grandkids a drink of water from the kitchen faucet.

In later years Malisa used a wooden walking cane to steady her balance. In March 1961, as she was walking down the hallway of her home Melisa's fell. Landing on the hard wooden floor her left leg was broken in the accident. She was admitted to St. Anthony's Hospital in Oklahoma City. It was there she passed away on 28 March 1961. She is buried at Canute Cemetery next to husband George W. Gunter.

Gunter Family Christmas-1932
Top Row L-R: Vida, Nell, Hattie, Betty, and John,
Seated L-R: Rosie, Albert, George, Malisa, Ollie, and Bessie.

Children of Malisa & George Gunter

Albert Bruce Gunter Family

Albert Bruce Gunter (Ab) was born 20 Feb 1892 in Chickasaw Nation Indiana Territory. According to documents completed by Ab he was born near Ardmore, Oklahoma.

Before 1900 the Gunter family moved by covered wagon from their home in Indian Territory to Oklahoma Territory and settled upon a claim in an area known as Turkey Creek. Albert appears in the 1900 Federal Census living with his parents on Turkey Creek, Washita County, Oklahoma Territory, where he assisted his father with farming and raising livestock.

Ab is absent from the 1910 and 1920 Federal Censuses. He is found residing in New Mexico on 5 Jun 1917 where he registered for the draft of WWI while living in Sante Fe County. His Draft Registration Card states the following information: *Albert Gunter residing in Stanley, New Mexico was born Feb. 20, 1892 in Ardmore, Oklahoma, giving his age as 25. He lists Farmer as occupation stating he is self-employed near Stanley, NM. He is free of dependents, single, white, has no military experience and claims no exemptions from military draft. He is described as medium build with blue eyes and light hair. Information was given at Precinct 10, Sante Fe County, New Mexico.* (ancestry.com)

Around 1921 Albert married Ruby Lorene Paulson (known as Ruth). She was born near Snyder in Oklahoma Territory on 7 Jun 1905, the daughter of Clarence C and Celia Jane (Rury) Paulson. Albert and Ruby divorced.

In 1924 Ab had a brush with the local law enforcement for operating an illegal still.

The 1930 Federal Census states Albert and Ruby are living near Canute, Oklahoma. On Apr 8th they are residing in Turkey Creek Township and have the following children: Janie (Malisa Jane), Lathie (Philathia), Georgia (Irene), and Sylvia (Imogene). Living with them also were Albert's parents, George and Malisa Gunter, and his younger brother John. Albert is renting the home place from father George and lists occupation as farmer.

In the Texas Birth Records Index found at www.ancestry.com, it is recorded that in 1932 Albert Victor Gunter was born to Albert and Ruby Gunter living in Brownwood, Brown County, Texas.

Prior to 1935 Albert moved his family from Texas to a small town near Tulsa, Oklahoma. There he worked for the Standard Paving Company. Daughter Jeanne Gunter stated it was while the family was living there Ruby took the car and left. It took several days for her father to locate the automobile.

Albert and Ruby Gunter had the following children:
1. Malisa Jane Gunter
2. Philathia Bell Gunter
3. Georgia Paris Irene Gunter
4. Sylvia Lavelle Imogene Gunter
5. Albert Victor Gunter

Following Ruby's departure Albert packed up the children and took them to live with his parents. By 1940 Janie and Irene are living in Missouri with their mother and stepfather Earl Hill. Janie is listed in the census as a cousin to head of household and Irene is listed as Irene Hill, daughter to head of household. AV and Imogene have moved back with their father who has moved to Blaine County while Philathia remained with her Gunter grandparents.

Prior to the 1940 US Census Albert remarried. His wife, Clara A Pedersen was born in Kansas 10 Mar 1896. She was the daughter of Norwegian immigrants Ole G and Emma Pedersen of Kansas. Ab and Clare are residing in Geary, Blaine County, Oklahoma with children Imogene and AV. The census states that in 1935 Albert was residing in Ardmore, Oklahoma. Ab's son, AV Gunter's obituary states the family relocated to Geary, Oklahoma in 1936. In 1940 Ab owns his home and gives his occupation as a laborer. Additions to the family include a son, Gerald Gene Gunter born in 1937 and daughter Ola Claringa Gunter born in 1939.

In 1954 on 10 July Albert applied for a delayed birth certificate for his son Albert Victor Gunter. The birth application states Ab was employed as a team foreman for Standard Paving Company at the time his son Albert Victor was born in 1932.

In the late 1950s Albert developed stomach ulcers. In a letter written by his wife Clara to sister-in-law Ollie, she stated the ailment caused him distress and restricted his diet. Initially it was determined by his doctor it was not cancer.

A granddaughter, Ruby Menard stated she very briefly saw Albert once and remembered him as having bright orange red hair and a gentle, but stern voice.

On 5 Jan 1962 Albert B. Gunter passed away. He is buried at the Geary Cemetery just outside of Geary, Oklahoma in Blaine County. His wife Clara passed away on 18 Dec 1977. She is buried next to her husband at the Geary Cemetery.

Albert and Clara Gunter had the following children:
6. Gerald Gene Gunter
7. Ola Claringa Gunter

1.   MALISA JANE GUNTER named after her paternal grandmother was known in her childhood as Janie. She was born on 16 Jan 1922 in Canute, Washita County, Oklahoma.

In the 1930 Federal Census she is living with her parents and grandparents near Canute, Oklahoma. The 1940 Census indicates in 1935 she was living in Tulsa, Oklahoma. By 1940 she has moved to Missouri. In the census Janie can be found living in Ralls County with her mother Ruth and stepfather Earl Hill.

Taken from a copy of the marriage license, Malisa Jane Gunter married George E Rissmiller on 26 Jun 1940 in Ralls County, Missouri. George was the son of George S and Sula Mae (Lynch) Rissmiller. Malisa and George divorced.

Malisa and George Rissmiller had the following children:
    Georgia Lavelle Rissmiller
    Sula Lorraine Rissmiller

Janie married second a serviceman in the Navy, Glenn Edward Harlinger. He was born on 10 Jun 1922 in Missouri, the son of Glenn V and Olive S (Turnes) Harlinger. (ancestry.com)

Following the marriage Janie's two daughters took the surname Harlinger.

In a 1951 US City Directory published for Davenport, Iowa, Glenn E and M Jane Harlinger are living at 501 S Lincoln Avenue. Glenn is employed as a loader at Peter Pan Bakery.

The 1953 US City Directory published for Davenport, Iowa, Glenn E and Melisa J Harlinger remain at their Lincoln Avenue address. Glenn is manager of Dixie Cream Donut Shop. Mrs. Jane Harlinger is a helper at the Dixie Cream Donut Shop.

In 1954 the US Directory records Janie and Glenn remain in Davenport, Iowa at their Lincoln Avenue address. Glenn is employed as a Salesman for Harry J Craig. In 1955 he is listed in the directory as a salesman for Omar, Inc.

In the 1956 US City Directory Glenn E and Malisa are listed as living in Rock Island, Illinois. The given address is RD 1 Eldridge, Iowa. Glenn is employed as an apprentice for Reynolds Engineering. Mrs. Malisa J Harlinger is employed at Continental Baking as a bake icer.

In later years Glenn E Harlinger was employed at an armory in Davenport, Iowa. By 1993 Malisa Jane and her husband Glenn are indexed as living in Bettendorf, Iowa. The index later indicates they relocated to Milton, Florida.

Malisa Jane Harlinger passed away on 29 Aug 2003 in Milton, Santa Rosa County, Florida. Her husband Glenn passed away 20 Dec 2003 in Milton, Florida. (ancestry.com)

Malisa and Glenn Harlinger had the following children:
    Delores Ann Harlinger
    Glenn Edward Harlinger, Jr.
        Mary Malisa Harlinger
        Zachary Glenn Harlinger

2. PHILATHIA BELL GUNTER, referred to as Phil was born on 1 Apr 1924 in Canute, Washita County, Oklahoma. Philathia's personality has been described as quiet and reserved.

Phil lived with her elderly Gunter grandparents in Custer County, Oklahoma, assisting with their care. She remained in the household until the death of her grandfather in 1943. Following her grandfather's demise she relocated to Oklahoma City.

From a copy of the marriage license, Philathia Bell Gunter married Leon Roper on 12 Aug 1944 in Oklahoma City, Oklahoma County, Oklahoma. Mr. Max Stanfield, minister of the Immanuel Baptist Church in Oklahoma City performed the ceremony. Present were Ruth M Adair and Phil's sister, Imogene Gunter. Leon Roper was the son of John Emery and Esther Caroline (Turney) Roper of Stigler, Haskell County, Oklahoma. Philathia and Leon divorced.

On 10 Nov 1945 husband Leon enlisted as a Private in the US Army at Chaunalt Field, Illinois. Enlistment was for the Panama Canal Department. Source of information is found at ancestry.com, 'Enlisted Man, Philippine Scout or Recall to AD of an enlisted man who had been transferred to the ERC'. Marital status at time of enlistment is given as married.

The 1948 US City Directory published for Muskogee, Oklahoma lists Philathia B Roper residing at 831 Creek Street. She is employed as a packer at Brockway Glass Company. The 1950 Muskogee City Directory lists Mrs. Philathia Roper residing at 615 S Cherokee.

Philathia and Leon Roper had the following children:
  A. Glenna Sue Roper
  B. Robert Leon 'Bobby' Roper

  A. Glenna Sue Roper was born 20 Aug 1945 in Oklahoma. She married Wiley Lee Hamilton on 19 Sep 1961 in Stanislaus County, California. Wiley was born on 2 May 1941 in Oklahoma, the son of Louis Floyd and Ruby Jewel (Doshier) Hamilton. He passed away on 30 May 1983 in Modesto, Stanislaus County, California.
  Published in the *Modesto Bee* on Feb. 13, 2014, Glenna Sue Hamilton died 2 Feb 2014 in Modesto, Stanislaus County, California.
  Glenna and Wiley Hamilton had the following children:
      Wiley Lee Hamilton, Jr.
      Phillip L Hamilton
      Linda S Hamilton

  B. Robert Leon Roper was born on 23 Jun 1947 in Oklahoma. He married Glenda L Hill on 6 Aug 1965 in Stanislaus County, California. They divorced.
  Robert passed away on 17 May 1988 in Modesto, Stanislaus County, California.
  Robert and Glenda Roper had the following children:
      i. Sherry L Roper
      ii. Robert Leon Roper, Jr.

ii. Robert Leon Roper, Jr. was born on 23 Sep 1967 in Stanislaus County, California. He passed away on 14 Jun 1991 in Stanislaus County, California.

While living in Muskogee Philathia married second Lewis Glenn Geesman (known as Glenn L. Geesman). He was born in Oklahoma on 15 Sep 1925, the son of West and Bertie E Geesman. Philathia and Glenn married in Sebastian County, Arkansas on 6 Jan 1951. (ancestry.com)

In the 1952 US City Directory published for Muskogee, Oklahoma, Glenn L and Phil Geesman are residing at 415 North N Street. Glenn is employed as a driver.

In a 1954 obituary published for Phil's brother Albert Victor Gunter, it states Philathia and Glenn are still residing in Muskogee, Oklahoma.

In 1956 the US City Directory published for Modesto, California, it lists Phil B and Glenn L as living at 1217 Sam Avenue. Glenn is employed as a driver.

In the 1958 US Directory published for Modesto, California, Glen L and Philathia Geesman are residing at 626 Empire Avenue. Glenn is a driver for Swede Jenson.

In 1959 the US Directory published for Modesto, California, Glenn and Philaphia Geesman remain at the Empire Avenue address. Mrs. Philaphia Geesman is employed as an inspector at Gallo Glass. In 1960 Philathia and Glenn remain on Empire Avenue and Phil continues employment at Gallo Glass.

In an email dated 2 Mar 2014 from grandson Vincent Geesman, he wrote, "From what I remember of my grandma she was really nice. She always gave me candy when I came over. …I do remember she would read books every day."

Philathia passed away on 23 June 2005 in Modesto, Stanislaus County, California. She is buried at Lakewood Memorial Park in Hughson, California. (findagrave.com).

Philathia's obituary published in *The Modesto Bee* (Jun/26/2005) states "…while residing in Modesto, she was employed as a quality assurance officer at Gallo Glass Co. and spent a portion of her free time volunteering at the Memorial Medical Center. She had thirteen grandchildren and ten great-grandchildren."

Philathia and Glenn Geesman had the following children:
   C. Mary R Geesman
   D. Edward Glenn Gessman

   C. Mary R Geesman was born in 1951 in Oklahoma.
      In Stanislaus County, California on 18 Nov 1966 she married Charles Boyd Shirley.
      Charles was born in 1948 in Kern County, California. They divorced.
      Mary and Charles Shirley had the following children:
         i. Charles P Shirley born 23 Apr 1967 in Stanislaus County, California. He died 1 Jun 1967 in Stanislaus County, California. (ancestry.com/California Birth and Death Index)
         ii. Cheryl Lynn Shirley Chin (ancestry.com/California Birth and Death Index)

Mary married Bruce William Chin. (ancestry.com/California Marriage Index)

D. Edward Glenn Geesman was born 1956 in Stanislaus County, California (ancestry.com/ California Birth Index).

Edward married Sabrina Costello on 2 Jul 1977 in State Line, Douglas County, Nevada. (ancestry.com/Nevada Marriage Records) The marriage record was filed in Carson City, Nevada on 15 Jul 1977, Book 79, Pg. 248. They divorced.

Edward married Robin Ann Hubbard.

Edward and Robin Geesman had the following children:

    i. Vincent Raymond Geesman
        a. Trinity Rowan-Jean Geesman born in Louisiana on 7 Dec 2011 and passed away 25 Dec 2012 in New Orleans, Orleans Parish, Louisiana.
    ii. Melissa Nichole Geesman
    iii. Chad Keith Geesman

3. GEORGIA PARIS IRENE GUNTER (Irene) was born near Canute, Oklahoma on 3 May 1926. Daughter Ruby Menard described her mother as strong-willed, hardworking, and independent, adding she possessed a feisty personality. Ruby remembers her mother having beautiful dark hair with red highlights that in the sun looked like diamonds sparkling in her hair. Irene also had green eyes.

In the 1930 Federal Census Georgia is living with parents Albert and Ruby near Turkey Creek in Washita County, Oklahoma. Also living in the household are siblings Janie, Philathia, and Imogene, her Uncle John and Gunter grandparents.

In the 1940 Census Georgia is found in Missouri living with her mother Ruth and stepfather Earl Hill. She is listed as Irene Hill. The census states she has completed the 7th Grade and in 1935 was residing in Tulsa, Oklahoma.

Irene married first William Potter. They divorced.

Irene married second Charles Henry Stringer on 30 Dec 1941 in Caraway, Craighead County, Arkansas. They divorced.

Ruby stated her parents Charles and Irene settled on a 360-acre farm raising cotton until hard times hit and they lost the farm. The family relocated to a home high on a mountain. Ruby remembers the house, the barn, the gardens her mother raised, their animals, and the cellar belonging to the place, stating she had such happy times there.

In February 1950 a heavy snow fell. The winter storm disabled electrical power to the mountain home. Following restoration of electricity the wiring shorted, catching the home on fire. Irene hitched the mule to a sled, loaded up her 6 mo. old son and 7 year old daughter and then started down the hazardous mountainside. During the flight to safety, Irene endured extreme cold temperatures that almost caused the loss of a leg while trying to get her children to a neighbor's home. It took several months for her recover from bodily damage the cold inflected on her extremities.

Following the unfortunate destruction of her mountain home, the family moved into town, living in Bald Knob. Husband Charles continued employment as a truck driver.

Irene and Charles Stringer had the following children:
   A. Ruby Willene Stringer
   B. Henry Eugene Stringer

In the 1953 US City Directory published for Davenport, Iowa, Irene is listed as Mrs. Irene Stringer. She is residing with her sister Jane at 501 S Lincoln Avenue. Irene is employed as a helper at the Dixie Cream Donut Shop managed by brother-in-law Glenn.

In 1954 the US Cities Directory lists Irene G and Charles R Harlinger as residing in a basement dwelling located at 626 W 3rd Street in Davenport, Iowa. Charles is employed as manager of Park Grill Café.

Around 1955 Irene and Charles relocate to Oklahoma. While living there daughter Roberta Charlene Harlinger was born. Charles was employed as a chef at the Biltmore Hotel in Oklahoma City.

Not staying long in Oklahoma, Irene and Charles head for Texas where they live in Odessa and Brownsville. Charles finds employment in the oil fields. Daughter Ruby remembers the family living in a large beautiful house where her mother worked long and hard sanding and waxing the wooden floors to get them perfect. Soon after completing the tedious task a sandstorm kicked up and covered the floors with sand.

By 1957 Irene has relocated to California. For a while she, Charles and children reside with her mother and stepfather, Ruth and Earl Hill. Irene and Charles are listed in the 1957 edition of the US City Directory published for Modesto, California as residing at 3617 Railroad Avenue. Charles is employed as a cook at Mehagans.

In 1958 the US City Directory published for Modesto, California lists Irene as Mrs. Irene G Harlinger residing at 1829 Dallas Street. In the 1959 publication Irene is listed as Irene Harlinger residing at RD #1 Box 802 in Ceres. By publication of the 1960 US City Directory for Modesto, California Irene has resumed the name Stringer and is listed as Mrs. Irene G Stringer residing at 708 E Hatch Road.

Irene and Charles Harlinger had the following children:
   C. Roberta Charlene Harlinger
   D. Olive Jeanette Harlinger

Following the divorce from Charles, Irene reconnects with a childhood sweetheart. Prior to their meeting Ned Bowman had recently become a widower. Irene and Ned marry and later divorced. Daughter Ruby said that following the divorce her mother swore off men

Living in Tennessee Irene met William E Murphy, known as Doc. It is stated by daughter Ruby that William found Irene rather than her looking for him. William lived on a large property near Jolten where he raised fruit trees. He has been described as a wonderful man in every respect. Irene called Ruby asking her to plan the wedding. Irene and William were married on 17 May 1974 in Jolton, Cheatham County, Tennessee.

Nephew Glenn Harlinger Jr. stated in an email dated 13 Mar 2013 that in later years Irene lived in Franklin, Kentucky on a farm a few miles out of town.

Daughter Ruby described her mother as very artistic and great at multitasking. While living in Kentucky Irene worked as a registered caregiver. Following the death of her husband William Murphy, she was employed for several years at a florist shop. While working there Irene was known for the artistic arrangements she created. During her lifetime Irene had also been an employee at Dale Kates, Incorporated where she worked as a seamstress.

Irene's obituary states that Georgia Irene Murphy passed away on 18 Aug 2000 at her home near Franklin, Warren County, Kentucky. She had 15 grandchildren and 17 great-grandchildren. Irene is buried at Woodburn Cemetery, Woodburn, Kentucky.

A. Ruby Willene Stringer was born in 1942 in Missouri. She was named Ruby after her maternal grandmother Ruby Hill and Willene after her mother's first husband, William. Ruby stated that when she was young, she was a toe-head with green eyes.

After fire burned their mountain home, Rudy relocated with her family into town. While living in Bald Knob she remembers attending Phillips 66 School, a one-room schoolhouse. She stated it was there she had the fondest memories of school. She enjoyed gymnastics and remembers participating in a local parade.

Ruby married Alfred J Menard, Jr. on 11 Oct 1960 in Stanislaus County, California. Alfred was born 12 Sep 1939 in San Diego, San Diego County, California, the son of Mr. and Mrs. Alfred J Menard. Alfred's nickname for Ruby was 'Irish'. Ruby refers to her husband as 'Papa'.

Ruby and Alfred soon relocated to Florida. In time Ruby found herself unhappy living in an urban environment. Longing for country life, she purchased a tract of land near Cantonment in Escambia County, Florida. Ruby stated it was the first tract sold on the first day of sales in the new subdivision. The property situated on a mountain top was purchased on 31 Oct 1966. As she put it, "I thought I wanted to be a city slicker but ended up on a piece of property to far in the sticks."

After purchasing the parcel of land Ruby wasted no time preparing for the move. When her husband arrived home from work that night Ruby had a trailer hitched to her car and was loading personal belonging. At one o'clock in the morning she and her family headed for their new home. It became their permanent residence. It is where she raised her four children, milked the family cow twice daily, churned butter, and grew a two acre garden.

On the day Ruby purchased her mountain property, a tornado touched down damaging the school where her son was to attend a fall festival that evening. In 2004 during Hurricane Ivan a tornado formed from the storm, destroying the upper story of Ruby's large Colonial home. During the event Ruby, one of her daughters and a grandchild sheltered in a lower level bathroom until the storm passed. Losing the upper story during the tornado, Ruby's home was damaged beyond repair.

During a phone conversation Ruby proudly stated she was married 42 ½ years before her husband Alfred passed away. Ruby and Albert have four children she describes as strong-willed, independent, and extremely multi-talented. All are managers in their chosen fields of profession and are known as workaholics. As she phrased it, "I have 9 grandchildren and 13 great-grandchildren all living and warring on the mountain property I purchased in 1966 as their home."

Ruby's husband Alfred passed away on 17 Jan 2002 in Escambia County, Florida. He is buried at Eastern Memorial Gardens in Pensacola, Escambia County, Florida.

Following the death of her husband, Ruby's doctor suggested she do something she had always wanted to do. Ruby enrolled at Pensacola Junior College having in mind a degree in early childhood development. Even though she did not get to complete her degree, Ruby stated she had a ball while there.

Ruby worked as a licensed seamstress for more than 20 years, designing and making wedding dresses and much more.

Ruby and Alfred J Menard, Jr. had the following children:
   i. Alfred John Menard III
   ii. Karen Esther Menard
   iii. Kathyren Elizabeth Menard
   iv. Allen Joseph Menard

   i. Alfred John Menard III was born in 1961 in California. He married Shelly Ann Story in Escambia County, Florida on 6 Dec 1980. They divorced.
     John married second Deborah Dianne Way on 3 Aug 1992 in Escambia County, Florida.

     Alfred John and Debbie Menard had the following children:
       a. Alfred John Menard IV
       b. Ericka Leanne Menard
   ii. Karen Esther Menard was born in 1969. She married David Glen Brogan, Jr. on 24 Oct 1989 in Escambia County, Florida. They divorced. They had no children.
     Karen married second Clifford Kenneth Baggett, Jr. on 11 Jun 1991 in Escambia County, Florida. They divorced. They had no children.
     Karen married third Keith Allen Bryant on 24 May 1996 in Escambia County, Florida. They divorced.
     Karen and Keith Bryant have the following children:
       a. Keith Bryant, Jr. (KJ)
       b. Linda Dianne Bryant
   iii. Kathryn Elizabeth Menard, known as Kathy married her high school sweetheart, James Simmons. For the garden wedding her mother Ruby made the bride's dress as well as dresses for the attendants. Kathy is an architect. She and her husband James own and operate a construction company.
     Kathy and James Simmons have the following children:
       a. William Earl Murphy Simmons (Doc)
       b. Helen Simmons

      iv. Allen Joseph Menard has three sons:
          a Jeff Menard
          b. Alex Menard
          c. David Menard

          b. Alex Menard married his only childhood sweetheart. They were engaged since 4th grade. They have two sons nicknamed Looney and Tuney.

B. Henry Eugene Stringer, nicknamed Hank was born in 1949 in Arkansas. Sister Ruby stated that Henry served five tours of duty in Viet Nam as a surgical nurse working in Medevac. Leaving the medical field, he transferred his military occupation to tanks, spending 28 years in the military prior to retiring. After leaving the service Henry completed a teaching degree, then spent many years employed in the education field.

C. Roberta Charlene Harlinger, nicknamed Charlie was born around 1955 in Oklahoma. Ruby stated she was given opportunity to name her baby sister she was so proud to have but was slow in coming up with a name. Before she could decide her mother named the new baby sister. Roberta married Alvin Ralph Sutton. They divorced.
Roberta married Ronald Dwayne Logan 30 Mar 1991 in Sumner County, Tennessee.

D. Olive Jeanette Harlinger was born in 1957 in California. Referred to as Jeanette, she stayed several years with older sister Ruby in Florida then returned to live with her mother. She later moved to Nashville, Tennessee.
Olive Petty married Edward Allen Evens 5 Jan 1980 in Sumner County, Tennessee. They divorced.
Olive Evens married Tommy Allen Rice on 11 Feb 1995 in Washoe County, Nevada.

  4. SYLVIA LAVILLE IMOGENE GUNTER was born 1928 in Canute, Washita County, Oklahoma. In childhood she was called Imogene or Sylvia.

After her father married Clara Pedersen, Jeanne moved to Geary to live with her father. It was there she started the first grade.

In speaking with Jeanne she remarked that when she was young and the family went to visit her Gunter grandparents the drive seemed to take forever from Geary to the Gunter farm. What she remembered most about the journeys was the car bouncing and chugging along the highway.

The family later moved to a farm 2-3 miles from her Gunter grandparents. Jeanne lived on the farm a few years and then at age 15 moved to Oklahoma City to live with her sister Philathia.

Jeanne married James R Garvin on 17 Jan 1946 in Sebastian County, Arkansas. (ancestry.com/Arkansas Marriage Records). They divorce.

Jeanne and James moved to Wisconsin and later to California. The 1954 edition of US City Directory published for Modesto, California lists Jeanne and James living in Modesto, California.

Jeanne and James Garvin had the following children:
- A. James 'Jim' Garvin
- B. Patricia Garvin
- C. Sandra J Garvin
- D. Charles 'Chuck' Garvin

C. Sandra Garvin, known as Sandy was born 9 May 1950 in Kenosha, Wisconsin. She married Paul Bergthold Sr. on 10 Nov 1968 in Davenport, Iowa. Sandra passed away 23 Nov 2011 in Davenport. (www.findagrave.com).

Sandra and Paul Bergthold had the following children:
- i. Angela Bergthold,
- ii. Tony Bergthold,
- iii. Michael Bergthold

D. Charles Garvin, nicknamed Chuck was born in 1951 in Wisconsin. He married Anita Diane Huff. She was born in 1951 in Illinois.

Charles and Anita Garvin have the following children:
- i. Patrick Wayne Garvin born in 1975 in Illinois. He married Emma Kay Kruse born in 1977 in Iowa.

    Patrick and Emma Garvin have the following children:
    Race James Garvin born in 2004 in Iowa.
- ii. Stephen James Garvin born in 1983 in Illinois.

Jeanne married Johnny Ray Gunter on 17 Jun 1957 in Modesto, California. (ancestry.com/California Marriage Index) Johnny Ray was born 3 Jun 1934 in Canute, Washita County, Oklahoma, the son of John and Avo (Wilson) Gunter. He passed away on 13 Mar 2007 in Carbon Cliff, Illinois and is buried at the Rock Island National Cemetery in Rock Island, Illinois.

Jeanne stated that soon after she and Johnny married he was transferred to a military installation in Pasco, Washington. It was while living there a son, Johnny Ray, Jr. was born.

Jeanne stated she spent life busy as a housewife and mother, and that she and Johnny were very involved with their church.

Jeanne and Johnny Ray Gunter had the following children:
Johnny Ray Gunter, Jr.
Jonathan Gunter

5. ALBERT VICTOR GUNTER (known as AV) was born on 15 May 1932 in Brownwood, Brown County, Texas.

Following his parents' separation AV went to live with his Gunter grandparents. In 1936 he moved to Geary, Blaine County, Oklahoma to live with his father and stepmother.

Albert Victor attended Geary High School, quitting prior to graduation. He completed his education while serving his country. After his father relocated to the a farm, AV helped with chores and farming.

AV enlisted in the US Army in January 1948 and reenlisted on 2 Feb 1951. He completed Basic Training at Fort Jackson, South Carolina and then spent two years at Fort Sill, Oklahoma training in field artillery. Following training he served a three-year tour of duty overseas stationed in Babenhouseun, Germany. AV was assigned as a light equipment operator. He obtained the rank of Sergeant a month before his death. (Albert Victor Gunter obituary)

AV was killed in Germany on 16 Feb 1954. His death was a result of a truck accidentally backing onto him, wedging his body against another truck. It was said he initially laughed off the incident but died later that day from injuries. His service number was RA18279873. At time of death he was attached to SVC Battery, 18th Field Artillery Battalion.

AV is buried next to his father in Geary Cemetery in Geary, Blaine County, Oklahoma.

AV never married and had no children. .

6. GERALD GENE GUNTER was born in Oklahoma City, Oklahoma County, Oklahoma on 24 Oct 1937. He was raised in Geary and graduated from Geary High School in 1956. During school years he was referred to as 'Red'. Gerald was active in sports, lettering in baseball, basketball, and football. His wife Betty said Gerald loved baseball most and was a very good at it.

Gerald, known as Jerry enlisted in the US Navy on 30 May 1956. He was assigned to the USS Salem from 1956 to 1958. On 10 Jul 1959 he was discharged from duty. (ancestry.com/Military Records). Rather than return to civilian life, Gerald reenlisted and served until July 1962.

Gerald married Linda Lou Glidewell. Linda was born 5 Aug 1941, the daughter of ? and Ruby Glidewell. Linda passed away 15 Oct 1966. She is buried at Geary Cemetery in Geary, Blaine County, Oklahoma.

Gerald and Linda Gunter had the following children:
   A. Shawn Marie Gunter
   B. Tonya Mae Gunter
   C. Jeryl Ann Gunter

The 1967 US Public Records Index found on ancestry.com lists Gerald as living in Sparks, Nevada.

Gerald married Betty F. Dagostaro on 27 Nov 1969 in Los Angeles, California. (ancestry.com/ California Marriage Index 1960-1985) Betty was born in Maryland, the daughter of Italian parents, Sebastian and Mary (Urnisi) Dagostaro.

Gerald moved from Los Angeles, California to Reno, Nevada in 1977. The US Directory Index gives record of him living in Reno from 1996-1998.

Gerald was employed as a Citifare Bus driver for eight years. Prior to that he worked as a manager for an auto parts warehouse.

Loving sports, Gerald was an avid University of Oklahoma (OU) fan. He enjoyed following the university's football and baseball games, an interest he passed onto his daughters.

Gerald passed away on 8 May 1998 in Reno, Washoe County, Nevada. (www.findagrave.com)

Gerald and Betty Gunter had the following children:

D. Nicky Ann Gunter

A. Shawn Marie Gunter was born in 1963. After the loss of her mother she lived in Oklahoma with her aunt and uncle, Ola and Bud Harrington. Shawn adopted the surname Harrington. Moving to Nevada she attended Sparks High School.
Shawn married Frank P Martinez. on 16 Apr 1986 in Reno, Nevada. They divorced.
Shawn and Frank P Martinez had the following children:
   i. Frank Martinez, Jr.
Shawn married Leonardo P Quilao on 14 Feb 1993 in Washoe County, Nevada. Leonard was born in 1957 in Watonga, Philippines. They divorced.
Shawn and Leonard Quilao had the following children:
   ii. Athena Angelica Quilao
   iii. Veronica Alexandra Quilao

   i. Frank and Jenni Martinez, Jr. have the following children:
      James Martinez
      Desmond Martinez
   ii. Athena Quilao married Brad Kabfleishch in Nevada.
B. Tonya Mae Gunter was born in 1964 in Oklahoma. Early years were spent living in Oklahoma. In her early teens Tonya moved to Nevada. She graduated Sparks High School in Sparks, Nevada. Tonya and her sister Shawn are both accomplished seamstresses.
Tonya is with Nicholas Keen. Nicholas was born in 1961 in Nairobi, Kenya, Africa.
Tonya and Nicholas have the following children:
      Jake Keen
      Garrett Keen
C. Jeryl Ann Gunter was born 26 Dec 1965. She was named Jeryl after her father and nicknamed Jerri. Sister Tonya stated her father wanted three boys and got three girls. After the death of her mother, Jeryl was raised by her aunt Ola Harrington until reaching her teen years. While living with the Harrington family she adopted the surname.
Jerri married Kenneth Lee Rule in Washoe County, Nevada on 19 Aug 1993. They divorced.
Jerri was employed as a Keno waitress.
Jeryl passed away on 1 Mar 2004 in Reno, Washoe County, Nevada. She is buried with her parents at Geary Cemetery, Geary, Blaine County, Oklahoma.
Jeryl Ann Gunter/Harrington had the following children:
      Krystal
      Kristopher
D. Nicky Ann Gunter was born in 1971 in California. She attended school in Reno, Nevada,

graduating in 1989. Nicky married James Barmettler in Reno, Washoe County, Nevada on 27 May 1989. Like her father, she is a fan of OU football and baseball. Nicky enjoys traveling and the hobby of scrapbooking.

Nicky and James Barmettler have the following children:
    Haley Jewel Barmettler

Haley Jewel Barmettler was born in Nevada in 1993. She married Colten Edwards in Montana.

7. OLA CLARINGA GUNTER was born on 13 Apr 1939 in Geary, Blaine County, Oklahoma. In her baby book Godparents are listed as Lissie Gunter and G.W. Gunter.

Raised in Geary, Ola graduated Geary High School in 1957. After completing high school she relocated to Oklahoma City.

The name of Ola's first husband is unknown. They divorced.

    A. Leesa Jana Jones

In a US City Directory for Oklahoma City, Oklahoma published in 1961 she is listed as Ola Harrington. The index lists multiple addresses for previous residences in the city.

After the death of her sister-in-law Linda Gunter, Ola raised her brother Gerald's three young girls until they were teenagers.

In Texas Marriage Records (ancestry.com) Ola C Gunter and Walter H. 'Bud' Harrington married 24 Feb 1969 in Cooke County, Texas. Bud was born 13 Sep 1921, the son of Walter H. and Ellen Wave (Clark) Harrington. Bud passed away on 26 Aug 2007 in Canadian, Pittsburg County, Oklahoma. He is buried at Fort Gibson National Cemetery, Fort Gibson, Muskogee County, Oklahoma. Bud was a truck driver by profession.

Ola, Bud and children enjoyed many family vacations. On a trip to Mexico the family visited the ancient pyramids. Another vacation they toured Canada. Ola and Bud owned a boat and properties at Lake Eufaula where the family enjoyed fishing, boating and swimming.

During holidays Ola prepare large family meals. Daughter Itha Harrington stated that dinner guests often included aunts Betty Miller and Bessie Brown .

Ola was employed as a sky chef at Will Rogers Airport in Oklahoma City.

Ola passed away on 15 Nov 1990 in Oklahoma City, Oklahoma County, Oklahoma. She is buried near her parents at Geary Cemetery in Geary, Blaine County, Oklahoma.

Ola and Walter Harrington had the following children:
    B. Terry Victor Harrington
    C. Itha Danette Harrington

A. Leesa Jana Jones/Harrington was born in 1959 in Oklahoma. She married Ernest James Wilmore, Jr. in Clark County, Nevada on 15 Jul 2000.
B. Terry Victor Harrington was born in 1961 in Oklahoma. He graduated from Southeast High School in Oklahoma City, Oklahoma. Terry is a licensed pilot and works for the FAA (Federal Aviation Administration). He has taught flight instruction and now serves as a supervisor.
C. Itha Danette Harrington graduated from Southeast High School in 1981. As a pastime she enjoys shopping and watching her sons participate in sports. Itha states she is a big OU Football fan.
Itha Harrington has the following children:
Amanda Harrington
Shirley Harrington
Ashley Harrington
Ricky Harrington
Christopher Harrington

Rosa Marie Gunter

ROSA MARIE GUNTER (known as Rosie) was born 23 Sep 1893 in Indian Territory near present day Hennepin, Oklahoma. Rosie has been described by grandson Ronald Lutes as being a strong willed, free spirited person prone to differences of opinion with her father. It was pointed out that both had red hair and were very much alike.

As a young girl Rosie's family moved from Homer, Indian Territory to Washita County, Oklahoma Territory. Living there she attended school completing the 8th grade. (ancestry.com/1940 US Census)

Grandson Ronald Lutes said that Rosie met her future husband David Nelson as he was working his way home from California after being discharged from the military. As he was passing through Canute her father George hired him as a farm laborer. Rosie and David were married on 21 Jun 1914 in Canute, Washita County, Oklahoma. David Joel Nelson was born on 7 Feb 1891 in Montgomery County, Indiana, the son of John L and Nancy Adeline (Largent) Nelson.

On 5 Jun 1917 David registered for the draft of World War I. His draft registration card filed in Crawfordsville, Montgomery County, Indiana states that he and Rosa have one child. It is noted on the registration he had previously served 3 years in the Coast Artillery (Regular Service) and another 3 years in the 13 Calvary. At time of registration he was employed as a farmer. (ancestry.com/U.S., World War I Draft Registration Cards, 1917-1918) David Nelson's obituary states he was a WW I veteran.

The 1920 US Census found online at ancestry.com shows Rosie and David living in Detroit, Wayne County, Michigan with daughter Gertrude listed as born in 1915 in Oklahoma and son Robert listed as born in 1919 in Michigan. On 2 Jan they are residing at 39 Marcy Street in Detroit. David is employed at a car factory.

In 1924 the US City Directory published for Lafayette, Indiana lists Rosa and David J Nelson residing at 1626 Union Street. David lists occupation as laborer.

In 1925 Rosa and David have a son, David J Nelson, Jr. born in Elk City, Beckham County, Oklahoma.

The 1926 US City Directory published for Lafayette, Indiana indicates Rosa and David J Nelson have returned to Indiana, establishing a residence at 15 S 6th Street. David lists occupation as laborer.

By 1929 Rosie and David have moved to Crawfordsville, Indiana where a daughter Blanche Nevada is born on 6 January.

The 1930 Federal Census states Rosie and David are renting a home in Crawfordsville, Montgomery County, Indiana at 713 Chandler Lane. David continues to list his occupation as laborer..

On 24 January 1933 Rosa and David are residing at 607 Liberty Street, Crawfordsville, Indiana. On that date David is killed in a construction accident. He is buried at the Oak Hill Grant Avenue Cemetery in Crawfordsville, Indiana.

After the death of her husband, Rosie is found in the 1934 US City Directory for Oklahoma City, Oklahoma. She is on record as residing at 1404 S Robinson, a residence owned by brother-in-law Alfred Brown. In 1935 and 1936 Rosie with family are living at 307 SW 22 Street in Oklahoma City.

Remaining in Oklahoma City, the 1937-1939 publications of the US Cities Directory records Rosa M Nelson (widow of David J) as residing at 434 NW 6th Street.

By the 1940 US Census Rosa M Nelson has returned to Crawfordsville, Indiana. She and family are residing at 705 Chandlers Lane. Rosie is paying $10.00 a month rent and gives seamstress as her occupation. (ancestry.com/1940 Census)

The 1942 US Cities Directory published for Crawfordsville, Indiana gives record of Rosie continuing to reside at the Chandler Lane address.

The 1944 US City Directory for Crawfordsville, Indiana indicates Rosa M Nelson (widow of David J) has again relocated, this time she and her family have returned to the house located at 607 Liberty Street. The directory lists her employed as a defense worker at Allison's.

Remaining at 607 Liberty Street in Crawfordsville, Rosa M Nelson is again found in the 1952 edition of US City Directory for Crawfordsville, Indiana. The directory lists her occupation as a bindery worker at Donnelley's. In the 1954 directory her address remains the same. Her occupation is listed as a pressman employed at Donnelley's. In the 1956 directory Rosie remains at 607 Liberty Street. The listing gives indication she has retired.

Niece Mary Ellen Stevens-Stewart once remarked that after the loss of her husband, Rosie financially supported her family working from home as a fortuneteller. In a phone conversation with grandson Ronald Lutes he verified this and stated his grandmother had clients who would come from all over the area seeking her service. Nancy Ammerman stated Rosie read the cards. Niece Jeanne Gunter told a story of when she was young she spent a week with her aunt. During the stay her cousins talked about their mother holding séances, but never in the home where they lived.

Struggling as a single parent affected by the Great Depression Rosie supported her family by various other means. Working from her home she provided a laundry service and often did seamstress work. In later years to supplement her income she rented the second story of her 607 Liberty Street home as an apartment.

In Crawfordsville Rosie sought employment at RR Donnelley & Sons Company. There she remained employed until deciding it was time for retirement.

Nancy Ammerman stated that Rosie loved to cook and was 'very good' at it.

Rosie remained at her home on Liberty street until deteriorating health gave cause to place her into an elderly care facility.

Rosa passed away on 24 Feb 1980 in Crawfordsville, Montgomery County, Indiana. She is buried next to her husband David at Oak Hill Grant Avenue Cemetery in Crawfordsville.

Rosa Marie Nelson's obituary states she was a member of the Pleasant View Baptist Church, a Gold Star Mother, and retired from R&R Donnelly and Sons.

Rosie and David Nelson had the following children:
1. Julia Gertrude Nelson
2. Robert Perry Nelson
3. George Lee Nelson
4. Marguerite Marie Nelson
5. David Joel Nelson, Jr.
6. Dorothy Mae Nelson
7. Blanche Nevada Nelson
8. Ernest James Nelson

1. JULIA GERTRUDE NELSON (known as Gertrude) was born 6 Apr 1915 in Oklahoma. During childhood life was spent alternating between Oklahoma and Indiana.

Julia married Albert Leslie Pickett on 6 Apr 1932 in Crawfordsville, Montgomery County, Indiana. Albert Leslie (known as Leslie) was born 26 May 1910 in Waynetown, Montgomery County, Indiana. He was the son of John and Georgia (Gray) Pickett. Leslie passed away in May 1974 in Crawfordsville, Montgomery County, Indiana.

In Alamo Julia owned and operated a grocery store for twelve years. Her obituary states that during her lifetime she was also employed for ten years by R.R. Donnelley and Sons of Crawfordsville.

Julia passed away on 9 Jul 1993 in Crawfordsville, Montgomery County, Indiana. She is buried at the Alamo Cemetery in Crawfordsville. In her obituary it is stated she had twenty-four grandchildren, forty-three great-grandchildren, and one great-great grandchild.

Julia and Leslie Pickett had the following children:
A. Donald Wayne Pickett
B. Ann Marie Pickett

C. David Leslie Pickett

D. George Duane Pickett

A. Donald Wayne Pickett (known as Don) was born 25 June 1934 in Crawfordsville, Montgomery County, Indiana. Don began his education at Alamo Public Schools and later attended Crawfordsville High School.

Don married Sherry Mae Witt. They divorced.

Don's obituary states he was self-employed in appliance repair. In addition he had worked at Pellet Mill and Allison's for several years.

Don passed away 26 May 2009 in Crawfordsville, Montgomery County, Indiana. He is buried at Oak Hill Cemetery North in Crawfordsville.

Don and Sherry Pickett had the following children:

    i. Kathryn SusAnne Pickett
    ii. Daniel Wesley Pickett
    iii. Connie Jean Pickett
    iv. Larry Wayne Pickett
    v. Gerald Alan Pickett
    vi. Donald Pickett
    vii. Dennis Eugene Pickett
    viii. David Scott Pickett

    i. Kathryn SusAnne Pickett was born in 1954 in Indiana. She married John Garvin Vance on 30 Dec 1972 in Crawfordsville, Montgomery County, Indiana. John was born in California in 1952, the son of Walter Addington and Nell Sue (Fleming) Vance. **
    ii. Daniel Wesley Pickett was born in 1966 in Indiana. He is a twin to Dennis Eugene. Daniel married Lois Ann Baker on 27 Jun 1987 in Crawfordsville, Montgomery County, Indiana. Lois was born in 1968 in Indiana, the daughter of Edgar L and Freda S (Crouch) Baker. Daniel and Lois divorced**
    Daniel and Lois Pickett have the following children:
        a. Kerri Daniele Pickett
    iii. Connie Jean Pickett was born on 30 Nov 1955 in Crawfordsville, Montgomery County, Indiana.
    Connie Jean Pickett and Steven Alan Baldwin applied for a marriage license on 1 Feb 1977. They married on 4 Feb in Crawfordsville, Montgomery County, Indiana. Steven was born in Indiana in 1953, the son of Lawrence E and Patricia Ann (Greene) Baldwin. **
    Connie passed away on 14 Dec 1988 in Crawfordsville. She is buried at Oak Hill Cemetery in Crawfordsville.
    iv. Larry Wayne Pickett was born in 1953 in Indiana. He married Brenda Jo Moore on 29 Dec 1973 in Crawfordsville, Montgomery County, Indiana. Brenda was born in 1956 in Indiana, the daughter of Lloyd Leon and Emma Jo (Wilson) Moore. **
    Larry and Brenda Pickett has the following children:

a. Michael Garrett Pickett

    v. Gerald Alan Pickett went by the nickname Jerry. He was born in 1958 in Indiana. Jerry married Jolene R Hocking on 20 Aug 1977 in Crawfordsville, Montgomery County, Indiana. Jolene was born in 1959 in Indiana, the daughter of Raymond J and Joyce Lorraine (Olson) Hocking. **

Jerry and Jolene Pickett had the following children:

        a. Joshua Allen Pickett

          Joshua and Amy Pickett had the following children:

            Sullivan Matthew Pickett

    vi. Donald Pickett

    vii. Dennis Eugene Pickett was born in 1966 in Indiana. He is a twin to Daniel Wesley Pickett. He married Lana Eileen Cope on 21 Nov 1987 in Crawfordsville, Montgomery County, Indiana. Lana was born in 1969 in Indiana, the daughter of Donald Eugene and Lois Eileen (Paris) Cope. Dennis and Lana divorced. **

Dennis and Lana Pickett had the following children:

        a. Kyle Wayne Pickett

        b. Brittney Lynnae Pickett

    viii. David Scott Pickett was born in 1968 in Indiana. He married Andrea Leigh Lesley on 27 Oct 1986 in Crawfordsville, Montgomery County, Indiana. Andrea was the daughter of James Allen and Frankie Lavon (Petry) Lesley. Andrea was born in 1968 in Indiana. David and Andrea divorced. **

David and Andrea remarried on 22 Apr 1990 in Crawfordsville, Montgomery County, Indiana. They divorced.**

David and Andrea Pickett have the following children:

        a. Stefanie Michelle Pickett

        b. Kristen Summer Pickett

        c. Sara Pickett

The *Crawfordsville Journal Review* published on 8 Feb 2008 gives record of David S Pickett and Erin L Rice applying for a marriage license in Montgomery County, Indiana. The 25 Mar 2008 edition of the *Crawfordsville Journal Review* published a marriage announcement for David and Erin (Rice) Pickett. Erin was the daughter of Milton and Mary Rice.

Dave and Erin Pickett had the following children:

        d. Emma Pickett

        e. Alexander Scott Pickett

**Information found online at http://history.cdpl.lib.in.us/vitals.html

B. Ann Marie Pickett was born in 1936 in Indiana.

   Ann married first Mr. Eutsler. They divorced.

      Ann and Mr. Eutsler had the following children:

      Dale Eutsler

   Ann married second Fred Wilbur Neff on 30 Sep 1978 in Montgomery County, Indiana. Fred was born 11 Mar 1926 in Jamestown, Boone County, Indiana, the son of Albert William 'Bert' and Sarah Maude (Stamper) Neff. Fred went by the nickname Doug. He passed away on 2 Oct 2007 in Indianapolis, Marion County, Indiana. Doug is buried at International Order of Oddfellows Cemetery in Jamestown, Indiana.

   C. David Leslie Pickett

   D. George D Pickett was born 22 Dec1932 in Crawfordsville, Montgomery County, Indiana. George married Johanna I unknown. They divorced.

    George passed away 21 Oct 1994 in Lafayette, Tippecanoe County, Indiana.

  2. ROBERT PERRY NELSON, son of Rosa and David Nelson was known as Bob. He was born on 2 Mar 1919.

In the 1938 US City Directory published for Oklahoma City, Oklahoma Robert is listed as residing with his mother at 434 NW 6th Street. His employment is given as a deliveryman. In the 1939 US City Directory published for Oklahoma City he is residing with his mother and continues employment at Pasco Drug Store as a deliveryman.

Robert enlisted in the US Army on 30 Jun 1939. He was a WW II veteran. (ancestry.com)

In the 1940 US Census Robert is stationed at Ft. Bliss in El Paso County, Texas. His occupation is given as Soldier in the US Army. His highest grade of education completed is given as high school two years. Robert states he was living in Oklahoma City, Oklahoma in 1935. He was discharged from the military on 26 Sep 1945.

Robert married Hattie Marie Baldwin on 28 Jul 1946 in Crawfordsville, Montgomery County, Indiana.

In the 1949 US Cities Directory published for Crawfordsville, Indiana Robert P Nelson with wife Hattie are residing at 809 Louise Avenue. Robert lists employment as a mechanic at Citizens Auto Company.

In the 1952 US City Directory published for Crawfordsville, Indiana Robert P Nelson and wife Hattie are residing at 607 ½ Liberty Street. Robert lists occupation as laborer, stating he is employed at Allison's in Indianapolis. In the 1954-1957 editions of the Crawfordsville Directory Robert P and wife Hattie remain at 607 ½ Liberty Street. Robert is employed as a machinist at Allison's in Indianapolis.

In the 1958 US City Directory Robert P. and wife Hattie remain on Liberty Street. The directory lists Robert employed as a driver for Dain Coal and Supply Company. In the 1959 edition, his occupation is given as laborer, employed at Hytex Brick.

Robert was later employed as a carpenter.

Robert P Nelson passed away on 24 Oct 1972 in Crawfordsville, Montgomery County, Indiana. He is buried at Oak Hill Grant Avenue Cemetery in Crawfordsville. (obituary)

Robert and Hattie Nelson had the following children:
A. George Nelson
B. Jack Lee Nelson
C. Robert Nelson, Jr.
D. Ethel Pearl Nelson
E. Sandra Kay Nelson
F. Nancy J Nelson
G. Martha Jean Nelson
H. Mary J Nelson

A. George Nelson
B. Jack Lee Nelson was born in 1952 in Indiana. He married Kathryn Pauline Harrington on 23 Aug
   1974 in Crawfordsville. Kathryn was born in 1954 in Indiana, the daughter of Leslie Ward and
   Betty Jean (Simmons) Harrington.** Jack and Kathryn divorced.
   Jack and Kathryn married a second time in Crawfordsville, Montgomery County, Indiana
   on 15 Jul 1976. **
   Jackie Lee married Margaret Elaine Hensel on 5 Feb 1978 in Darlington, Montgomery County,
   Indiana. Margaret was born 1958 in Indiana, the daughter of Bernard Louis and Evelyn Louise
   (Boots) Hensel. **
C. Robert 'Bobby' Nelson, Jr.
D. Ethel Pearl Nelson was born in 1947 in Indiana. She married Rex Dale Hall on 24 Nov
   1962 in Crawfordsville, Montgomery County, Indiana. Rex was born in 1943 in Illinois,
   the son of Glen Dale and Pearletta Rose Hall. **
E. Sandra Kay Nelson was born in 1950 in Indiana. She married Robert Dean Abney on
   1 Jun 1968 in Crawfordsville, Montgomery County, Indiana . Robert was the son of
   Neville and Lovetta (Jornigan) Abney. **
F. Nancy J Nelson
G. Martha Jean Nelson was born in 1959 in Indiana. She married Wallace Leon Rice on
   14 Feb 1975 in New Ross, Montgomery County, Indiana. Wallace Leon was born in 1955
   in Missouri, the son of Wallace and Carol (Martin) Rice. **
H. Mary J Nelson
   ** Information from copies of marriage records.

   3. GEORGE LEE NELSON, son of Rosa and David Nelson was born 20 Dec 1920 in Lafayette,
Tippecanoe County, Indiana.

In the 1939 US City Directory published for Oklahoma City George is living with his mother and
siblings at 434 NW 6th Street and lists employment as a clerk at Wes-Tel Drug Company.

George enlisted in the Oklahoma National Guard on 19 Sep 1940 at Oklahoma City, Oklahoma County,
Oklahoma. He was sworn into active duty in Jan 1943, serving with Headquarters Company 645th Tank
Destroyer Battalion.

George Lee Nelson married Ethel Pearl Feagins of McAlister, Oklahoma on Christmas Day 1941. She was known by the nickname Kitty. Ethel was born 8 Jan 1924 in Watonga, Blaine County, Oklahoma, the daughter of John E and Olivia Maude (Sykes) Feagins. She passed away 11 Jun 2001 in Abilene, Texas.

George's Oklahoma National Guard Division was deployed overseas 22 Jan 1943 to North Africa. The 45th Infantry Division entered combat on Sicilian soil in July. During the Naples-Foggia campaign in Italy on 22 Nov 1943 George was killed in action while guarding a prisoner. During WW II the Oklahoma 45th Infantry Division became known as the 'Fighting 45th'. George achieved the rank of Tec-4 prior to his death. His service number was 20825336. (ancestry.com/military)

George is buried at the Masonic Cemetery in Crawfordsville, Montgomery County, Indiana.

George and Ethel Pearl Nelson had the following children:
   Georgia Lee Nelson

   Georgia Lee Nelson was born in 1943 in Oklahoma. She attended Glen Oaks Senior High School in Baton Rouge, Louisiana. Georgia married Kenneth William Webster.
   Georgia and Kenneth Webster had the following children:
      Kenneth William Webster, Jr.
      James Matthew Webster

4. MARGURITTE MARIE NELSON daughter of Rosa and David Nelson was known as Margaret. She was born 14 Apr 1923 in Lafayette, Tippecanoe County, Indiana.

Margaret married Harry Elias Ammerman on 28 May 1941 in Crawfordsville, Montgomery County, Indiana. Harry was born on 1 Jan 1919 in Alamo, Montgomery County, Indiana, the son of Charles Lee and Bertha (Barkwell) Ammerman. In the 1940 edition of the US City Directory for Crawfordsville, Indiana Harry was employed as a pinsetter for Crawfordsville Bowling Alley.

In the 1942 US City Directory for Crawfordsville, Indiana Margaret and Harry are residing at 317 ½ E. College Street. Harry is employed as a mechanic at Combs Motor Service.

The 1944 US City Directory for Crawfordsville, Indiana has Margaret and Harry living at 509 Louisa. No record of employment is given.

In 1949 the US City Directory for Crawfordsville, Indiana records Margaret and Harry living at 903 Elmore Street. Harry profession lists as Auto Repair and he is employed at 1011 E. College Street.

The 1956 US City Directory for Crawfordsville, Indiana states Margaret and Harry are residing at 913 E Jefferson. Harry states he works as an auto repairman at his home address.

During the 1950s-60s Margaret was employed by Sommer Metalcraft in Crawfordsville, a wire manufacturing company.

Harry passed away 15 Apr 1993 in Crawfordsville, Montgomery County, Indiana. He is buried at Oak Hill Cemetery South in Crawfordsville.

Marguerite passed away on 3 Feb 2002 in Crawfordville, Montgomery County, Indiana. She is buried at the Oak Hill Cemetery South in Crawfordsville.

Marguerite and Harry Ammerman had the following children:
A. Harry Elias Ammerman, Jr.
B. Larry Joe Ammerman

A. Harry Elias Ammerman, Jr. was born in 1943 in Indiana. He married Nancy Carol Gibson of New Richmond, Indiana on 17 Dec 1960.
   Harry and Nancy Ammerman had the following children:
   i. Anthony Wayne Ammerman
   ii. Kenneth Duwayne Ammerman
   iii. Jeffery Alan Ammerman
   iv. Matthew Lee Ammerman

   i. Anthony Wayne Ammerman was born 26 Jan 1962 in Crawfordsville, Montgomery County, Indiana. Anthony's nickname was Tony. He married Deanna Marie Gilbert on 10 Aug 1985 at the Browns Valley Baptist Church in Montgomery County, Indiana. Deanna was the daughter of Lawrence and Lenora Mae (Landry) Gilbert of Colorado. Tony and Deanna divorced. **
   Anthony served in the US Army obtaining the rank of Spec-4.
   Tony enjoyed horses, fishing and racing go-carts.
   Anthony passed away on 9 Nov 1999. He is buried at Roachdale Cemetery in Roachdale, Putnam County, Indiana.
   Anthony and Deanna Ammerman had the following children:
        Angel Marie Ammerman
        Anthony 'Tony' Ammerman, Jr.
   ii. Kenneth Duwayne Ammerman was born in 1963 in Indiana. He was known by the nickname Kenny. Kenneth married Rhonda Jean Steele on 2 Feb 1985 in Crawfordsville, Montgomery County, Indiana. Rhonda was born in 1965 in Indiana, the daughter of James Richard and June (Rush) Steele. Kenny and Rhonda divorced. **
   Kenneth and Rhonda Ammerman had the following children:
        a. Cody Ammerman (twin to Coby)
        b. Coby Ammerman (twin to Cody)
        c. Kendra Ammerman
   Kenny married Kim ?. They divorced. Kenny and Kim Ammerman had no children.
   iii. Jeffery Alan Ammerman known as Jeff was born in 1966 in Indiana.
   Jeff and Holly Ammerman have the following children:
        Heather Ammerman
        Ashley Ammerman
   iv. Matthew Lee Ammerman nicknamed Matt was born in 1971 in Indiana.
   Matt has never married. He enjoys watching football and basketball games.
B. Larry Joe Ammerman was born in 1946 in Indiana. He married Wanda Lee Minnich on

26 Sep 1965 in Crawfordsville, Montgomery County, Indiana. Wanda was born in 1947 in Illinois, the daughter of Simon and Naomi (Rhoads) Minnich. **

Larry work as a self-employed mechanic and welder from 1970 to 1994. He then worked for Heritage Products as robotic welder. He is now retired. Wanda went to work for Culver Union Hospital in 1966 as a dishwasher and worked her way to supervisor at Culver AMI. She left Culver AMI in 1994 and is presently employed as a Food Service Supervisor.

Larry and Wanda Ammerman had the following children:

    i. Margaret Jane Ammerman

    ii. Larry Lee Ammerman

    iii. Carolyn Sue Ammerman

    i. Margaret Jane Ammerman was born in 1967 in Indiana.

    Margaret married Paul McDonald in Crawfordsville, Montgomery County, Indiana in 1990. They divorced.

    Margaret and Paul McDonald had no children.

    Margaret Ammerman is the mother of the following children:

        a. Aleta Ann Ammerman

        b. Dakota Layne Young

        a. Aleta Ann Ammerman was born in 1987 in Indiana. She graduated early in 2007 from South Montgomery High School in Crawfordsville, Indiana. Aleta enlisted in the US Marine Corp and trained at Paris Island, South Carolina. After training she was stationed in San Diego, California before a nine month deployment in Iraq. She was honorable discharged in 2011.

    ii. Larry Lee Ammerman was born 21 Aug 1969 in Indiana. He passed away on 30 Oct 1969. Larry is buried at Oak Hill Cemetery in Crawfordsville, Montgomery County, Indiana.

    iii. Carolyn Sue Ammerman was born in 1978 in Indiana. She married Anthony J. Walters in Aug 2003 in Montgomery County, Indiana. They divorced. **

    Carolyn and Anthony Walters had the following children:

        Desarae Ann Walter

    Carolyn is also mother to the following children:

        Marissa Loran

  **Information found on line at: http://history.cdpl.lib.in.us/vitals.html

5. DAVID JOEL NELSON, JR was born on 26 Feb 1925 at Elk City, Beckham County, Oklahoma.

In 1930 US Censuses David is listed in the US Census as living with his parents in Crawfordsville, Montgomery County, Indiana.

In the 1940 US Census David is living with his mother and siblings in Crawfordsville and is attending school.

David enlisted in US Army on 20 May 1943 at Indianapolis, Indiana and was discharged from service on 17 Mar 1946. David reenlisted in the US Army 18 Oct 1948 and was released on 13 Jul 1949. He was a veteran of WW II.

David married Marilyn Lou Runyun on 31 Dec 1949 at Crawfordsville, Montgomery County, Indiana. They later relocated to Gary, Indiana where David was employed by Republic Steel in South Chicago for 30 years.

David passed away 26 July 1997 at Crown Point in Lake County, Indiana. He is buried at Oak Hill Grant Avenue Cemetery in Crawfordsville, Indiana.

David and Marilyn Nelson had the following children:
A. Brenda Jean Nelson
B. Debra Lynn Nelson
C. Terry Dale Nelson

A. Brenda Jean Nelson was born in 1950 in Indiana. She attended Calumet High School in Gary, Indiana, graduating in 1968. Brenda married to Calvin Wiers in 1975 at the Trinity Reformed Church in Munster, Indiana.
Brenda and Timothy Wiers have the following children:
   i. Timothy Wiers
   ii. Michele Wiers
   iii. Michael Wiers

   i. Timothy Wiers was born and passed away in December 1975.
   ii. Michelle Wiers graduated in 1995 from Lake Central High School, Saint John, Indiana. She is a twin to brother Michael, Michelle being born first.
   iii. Michael Wiers graduated in 1995 from Lake Central High School, Saint John, Indiana. He is a twin to sister Michelle.
B. Debra Lynn Nelson (known as Debbie) was born in 1952 in Indiana. She graduated from Calumet High School.
Debbie married Theodore S (Ted) Czernoch on 24 Dec 1982. Ted was born in 1955 in Indiana. Debbie was a bus driver, retiring in December 2013.
Debbie and Ted Czernoch have the following children:
   Trisha Lynn Czernoch

   Trisha Lynn Czernoch was born 1982 in Indiana. In Aug 2013 she earned her Associate Degree.
   Trish is with Jeff Hylek. Jeff is employed as a lineman and often called to respond to and repair damages left in the wake of a storm.

   Trisha and Jeff have the following children:
   Haley Hylek
   Jenna Hylek

Debbie has been mother to two stepdaughters: Jennifer Lynn Czernoch (known as Jen) born in 1977 and Lisa Marie Czernoch born in 1975.

C. Terry Dale Nelson was born 8 March 1956 in Hammond, Lake County, Indiana. He graduated Calumet High School class of 1975. Terry was later employed at Metal Management as a crane operator. During free time he enjoyed camping, fishing and being with his friends.

Terry passed away 9 Jan 2005 in Gary, Indiana. He is buried at Oak Hill South Cemetery in Crawfordsville, Montgomery County, Indiana. (www.findagrave.com)

Terry has the following children:

Daniel Piddington

6. DOROTHY MAE NELSON, daughter of Rosa and David Nelson was known as Dot. She was born on 9 Mar 1927 in Lafayette, Tippecanoe County, Indiana. Nephew Ronald Lutes stated that her middle name Mae was derived from her maternal aunt, Vida Mae Gunter-Sanderson.

Dorothy married Charles Robert Lang on 18 Aug 1945.

In the 1949 US City Directory for Crawfordsville, Indiana Dorothy and C. Robert Lang are living at 607 ½ Liberty Street. The apartment is the second story of her mother Rosa's home. Robert is employed as an Ad Setter for R&R Donnelley & Sons.

In 1952 the US City Directory published for Crawfordsville, Indiana has Robert and Dorothy residing at 109 N. Grant Avenue. Robert is employed as a printer at Donnelley's. In 1954 and again in 1956 the US City Directory for Crawfordsville, Indiana records Charles R and Dorothy M Lang residing at 1008 Ray. In both records Robert is employed at Donnelley's as a press operator.

The 1958 and 1959 editions of the US City Directory published for Crawfordsville, Indiana Robert and Dorothy are living at 1111 Homewood Drive. Robert continues employment at Donnelley's working as a comptroller.

The US Public Records Index, Volume 2 gives residence for Dorothy M Lang at 550 Independence Highway, #N69, Inverness, Florida.

Charles Lang passed away on 26 Mar 1991 in Citrus County, Florida. He is buried at Oak Hill Grant Avenue Cemetery in Crawfordsville, Montgomery County, Indiana.

Dorothy passed away 27 Apr 2002 at the Citrus Memorial Hospital in Inverness, Florida. She is buried beside her husband at the Oak Hill Grant Avenue Cemetery in Crawfordsville, Montgomery County, Indiana.

Dorothy's obituary stated she owned and operated Dorothy's Beauty Shop and had been an employee of Holiday Inn and Sommer Metal Crafts in Crawfordsville. The obituary went on to say "Dorothy was an active member of the Christ Lutheran Church, Order of the Eastern Star, Culver Hospital Auxiliary, and the American Legion Auxiliary, serving several terms as President."

Dorothy and Charles Lang had the following children:
- A. Richard Leroy Lang
- B. Alan Jeffery Lang

- A. Richard Leroy Lang, known by the nickname Dick was born in 1946 in Indiana. He married Iris Delores Cauble on 13 Dec 1973 in Crawfordsville, Montgomery County, Indiana. Iris was born in 1950 in Indiana, the daughter of Ralph Wilson and Catherine Ann (Bieberich) Cauble. **
- B. Alan Jeffery Lang was born in 1957 in Indiana. He married Paula Ann Hughes on 12 May 1979 in Montgomery County, Indiana. Paula was born in 1954 in Indiana, the daughter of Dan Wesley and Ann (Saliens) Hughes. **

    Alan and Paula Lang had the following children:
    - i. Daughter Lang
    - ii. Wesley Danielle Lang

    **Information taken from http://history.cdpl.lib.in.us/vitals.html

7. BLANCHE NEVADA NELSON was the youngest daughter of Rosa and David Nelson. Known as Pat or Patsy, she was born on 6 Jan 1929 in Crawfordsville, Montgomery County, Indiana.

Blanche married Thomas Edwin Lutes. He was born 20 Jun 1923 in Indiana, the son of John and Ressa V Lutes. Blanche and Thomas divorced.

Blanche and Thomas Lutes had the following children:
- A. Danny Lee Lutes
- B. Ronald Eugene Lutes
- C. Gerold Dean Lutes
- D. Carl Edwin Lutes
- E. Karen Sue Lutes

Blanche married Howard Earl Bell on 26 Jun 1961 in Trosedale, Kentucky. Howard was born 15 Oct 1920, the son of Dode and Bertha (Myers) Bell. He passed away 27 Jan 2000 in Crawfordsville, Montgomery County, Indiana.

Published in her obituary, Blanche was employed 12 years at R.R. Donnelley and Sons Company in Crawfordsville.

Blanche passed away 9 June 1989 in Crawfordsville, Montgomery County, Indiana. She is buried at Oak Hill Cemetery in Crawfordsville.

Blanche and Howard Bell had the following children:
- F. Howard Earl Bell
- G. Catherine Bell
- H. Rebecka Sue Bell
- I. Raymond Everest Bell
- J. Daughter Bell

A. Danny Lee Lutes was born 28 Jul 1947 in Montgomery County, Indiana and passed away 30 Nov 1947 in Crawfordsville. He is buried at the Masonic Cemetery in Crawfordsville. (obituary)

B. Ronald Eugene Lutes was born in 1948 in Indiana. He married Dixie Earlene Bell on 30 April 1967 at Crawfordsville, Montgomery County, Indiana. Dixie was born in 1948 in Indiana, the daughter of Howard and Hazel Delores (Hubble) Bell. Ronald and Dixie divorced. **

Ronald and Dixie Lutes had the following children:

   i. Tanya Delores Lutes
   ii Thomas E Lutes

   i. Tanya Delores Lutes was born in 1968 in Illinois. She married Robert Dale Crouch on 4 May 1985 at Darlington, Montgomery County, Indiana. Robert was born in 1959 in Indiana, the son of Edmund and Marjorie L (Fox) Crouch. Tanya and Robert divorced. **

   Tanya and Robert Crouch had the following children:

       a. Fred J Crouch
       b. Brandon D Crouch

   Tanya married Jeffery A Johnson on 31 Dec 1992 in Crawfordsville, Montgomery County Indiana. Jeffery was born in 1966 in Indiana, the son of Larry L and Janise (Waye) Johnson. **

   ii. Thomas E Lutes was born in 1969 in Indiana. He married Bobbie Lillian Green on 9 Sep 1989 in Crawfordsville, Montgomery County, Indiana. Bobby was born in 1967 in Indiana. **

C. Garold Dean Lutes known as Gary was born in 1951 in Indiana.

D. Carl Edwin Lutes was born in 1953 in Indiana. He married Deborah Lynn Ward on 27 Jul 1973 in Crawfordsville, Montgomery County, Indiana. Deborah was born in 1955 in Indiana, the daughter of Larry Eugene and Myrna Delores Ward. Carl and Deborah divorced. *

E. Karen Sue Lutes was born on 28 Jan 1950 in Crawfordsville, Montgomery County, Indiana.
   Karen married Clyde Osborne. They divorced.
   Karen married John Linkhous.
   Karen and John Linkhous had the following children:
       John Linkhous, Jr.
       Tracy Linkhous
       Angel Linkhous
       Tammy Linkhous
   Karen passed away 6 Jun 1995. She is buried at Mount Pleasant Cemetery in Danville, Hendricks County, Indiana. (obituary)

F. Howard Earl Bell was born on Dec 1961 in Montgomery County Indiana. His obituary states that he died in infancy.

G. Catherine Bell, nicknamed Kathy was born in 1963 in Indiana.

Kathy married Ronald 'Ron' McCollum. **

H. Rebecka Sue Bell was born 1964 in Crawfordsville, Montgomery County, Indiana. Rebecka married Terry L Anderson on 3 May 1982 in Darlington, Montgomery County, Indiana. Terry is the son of Harold Franklin and Georgia Eleanor (Haskins) Anderson. **

I. Raymond Everest Bell was born Dec 1965 in Montgomery County, Indiana. His obituary states he died in infancy and is buried at Oak Hill Cemetery in Crawfordsville.

J. Daughter Bell was born Dec 1966 in Montgomery County Indiana. Her obituary states she and died in infancy. She is buried at Oak Hill Cemetery in Crawfordsville.

** Information from copy of marriage record.

8. ERNEST JAMES NELSON, known as Jimmy was the youngest son of Rosa and David Nelson. He was born on 17 Aug 1930 in Crawfordsville, Montgomery County, Indiana. He attended Crawfordsville Public Schools.

In the 1952 US City Directory published for Crawfordsville, Indiana Ernest J Nelson is residing with his mother at 607 Liberty Street. He lists employment as a janitor for Sommer Metalcraft. In the 1954 directory he remains with his mother and is employed as a factory worker at National Homes in Lafayette. The 1956 directory lists Jimmy living at home and employed as a driver for Goodman's Dept. Store. In the 1958 and 1959 directories Ernest is residing with his mother. No employment or occupation is listed.

In an email from Ronald Lutes dated 15 Jun 2012, Jimmy's nephew writes:

…(Jim) he was an avid fan of the Boy Scouts, and had two scouting handbooks that he read with great fervor.
…When he became old enough, he kept getting turned down by the Crawfordsville Police Dept. on becoming an officer. Grandma Nelson bought him a new 1957 Ford Custom which he added a mail order police siren under his hood. …leaving Crawfordsville he left his '57 Ford as it was in Grandma Nelson's name (she never learned to drive).
In the summer of 1960…he was part of a firefighting group trying to contain a large forest fire in Kings Canyon National Park.

After leaving Indiana Ernest is found on record as living in Bakersfield, California. In 1962 he married Frances Kaye Bock on 2 Jun in Kern County, California. Frances was born in 1944 in Ohio, the daughter of Paul J and Elsie (LeNarz) Bock. (Information from copy of marriage license.) Jim and Frances divorced.

In Montgomery County, Indiana Ernest J Nelson and Saundra (Ellis) Pierce applied for a marriage license on 8 Sep 1964. They were married on Sep 11th in Lafayette, Tippecanoe County, Indiana. Saundra was the daughter of Jack and Frances Priscilla Ellis. She was born 23 Oct 1938 in Houston, Harris County, Texas. Jim and Saundra divorced.

A family member's obituary published in 1972 states Jimmy is residing in Lakewood, Los Angeles County, California. In 1974 Ernest Nelson Jr. applied for a social security card listing California as the state of residence at time of issue.

Texas Marriage Records show Ernest James Nelson and Saundra Ellis remarried on 1 Oct 1978 in Ellis County, Texas. They later divorced.

In 1980 and again in 1989 it is published in a family member's obituaries that Ernest is living in Ferris, Texas.

A 1992 Public Directory Index (ancestry.com) lists Ernest residing in Ferris, Texas, and references him as having lived in Oklahoma City, Oklahoma. A cousin, Elmer Brown verified Jimmy with his family lived briefly in Oklahoma City.

Jimmy help raise Saundra's two daughters, Nelda Ruth Pierce born in 1963 and Peggy Renee Graham born in 1960.

Ernest and Saundra Nelson had the following children:
    A. Ernest James Nelson, Jr.
    B. Beverly Elaine Nelson

Ernest Nelson passed away 18 Dec 1992 in Huntsville, Walker County, Texas. In the Social Security Death Index (ancestry.com) it lists E Nelson's social security card issued before 1951 (Indiana). Last residence on record was Ferris, Texas.

A memorial page on Find-A-Grave.com lists Ernest Nelson as birthdate unknown with death 18 Dec 1992. The gravesite is located at Captain Joe Byrd Cemetery, Department of Corrections, Huntsville, Walker County, Texas-plot F-E-38.

    A. Ernest James Nelson, Jr. is recorded in the Texas Birth Index (ancestry.com) as born to Ernest J Nelson and Saundra Ellis in Houston, Harris County, Texas on 8 Dec 1964.
    Texas Marriage Records (ancestry.com) shows Ernie married Shalonda C Clements on 12 Aug 1988 in Dallas County, Texas. They divorce. (Texas Divorce Records/ancestry.com)
    Texas Marriage Index (ancestry.com) indicates Ernie and Shalonda remarried 9 Mar 1994 in Ellis County, Texas. They again divorced. (Texas Divorce Index /ancestry.com)
    Texas Birth Records (ancestry.com) gives record of two children born to Ernie and Shalonda Nelson:
        i. Chelsea Ann Nelson
        ii. Cortney Ann Nelson

    Texas Marriage Records (ancestry.com) shows Ernie married Linda L. Wisenberger on 4 Mar 2000 in Ellis County, Texas.

    A memorial page located on the website www.FindAGrave.com states Ernest James 'Ernie' Nelson passed away 2 Jun 2001. He is buried at Ferris Memorial Park North Cemetery in Ferris, Ellis County, Texas.

B. Beverly Elaine Nelson was born in 1969 in California.

Beverly married Frankie Doyle Teague on 21 Dec 1987 in Ellis County, Texas. They divorced.

Beverly and Frankie Teague had the following children:

    i. Samantha June Teague

    ii. Frank Travis Teague

Beverly had a daughter born in 1991 in Texas, Kathryn Nicole King.

Ollie Caroline Gunter

OLLIE CAROLINE GUNTER—Stated by Ollie she was born on 16 Sep 1895 near Davis, Oklahoma in what was known at the time as Indian Territory. (In 1895 'Oklahoma' was divided into Oklahoma Territory and Indian Territory. Oklahoma's statehood was still twelve years away.) The location of her birth points to being near Homer, Oklahoma.

Ollie is first found listed in the 1900 US Federal Census taken near Canute, Oklahoma Territory. Her father George states she was born in Indian Territory. Ollie told the story of when she was a little girl they moved from their home near Davis to Canute in a covered wagon. Soon after embarking on their journey Indians on horseback began following their wagon as they rolled across the prairie. Ollie said it was quite some time before the Indians turned back. In a biographical sketch submitted to the Lincoln County Historical Society, Mary Ellen Stevens-Stewart wrote that her mother moved to the Canute area at age 4.

Ollie told her grandchildren that when she was a young it was her chore to help with housework. She told of a time living in a home with dirt floors that she swept with a broom constructed from broomcorn. She spoke of growing up in the cotton fields hoeing, chopping and picking cotton and stated she never wanted to see another cotton field as long as she lived. Cotton was a valued source of family income.

Helping work the family farm and having restricted eyesight, Ollie's education was limited to finishing third grade yet she was able to read and write.

By 1926 Ollie has left the farm and Canute area. She is found in the 1926 US City Directory published for Oklahoma City, Oklahoma. While living in Oklahoma City she met Daniel Alexander Stevens, known as Dan or simply D.A. According to their daughter Mary Ellen, Ollie and Dan met while he was working as an agent for home and apartment rentals and Ollie was seeking a place to rent.

Contrary to what I was always told, and what Ollie's daughter published in the *History of Lincoln County* historical book, Ollie Gunter and Dan Stevens were not married on Valentine's Day. A copy of their marriage license and certificate shows Olive C Gunter and D. A. Stevens applied for a marriage license on 11 Feb 1928 and were married the same day. Daniel Alexander Stevens was born 2 Apr 1881 on a farm near Austin in Cass County, Missouri. He was the son of Albert and Mehatable (Hayden) Stevens. Daniel was married twice prior his marriage to Ollie. First to Cora June Reinoehl of Lebanon, Pennsylvania, and second to Mamie B. Roach, a widow living in Oklahoma City. Both marriages ended in divorce.

Ollie and Dan Stevens lived first in Oklahoma City where daughter, Mary Ellen was born 21 Jul 1929 at St. Anthony Hospital.

Around 1930 Ollie and Dan relocated briefly to Garden City, Missouri where they operated a restaurant.

Returning to Oklahoma Ollie and family lived for a short time in Geary until she and Dan purchased a farm south of Choctaw. After living on the Choctaw farm for three years Ollie and Dan returned to Oklahoma City.

Daughter Mary Ellen talked of how compassionate and giving her father was for others, especially during the Great Depression. She said her father was always one to help the less fortunate and told a story of the time he had purchased a new coat for her mother Ollie. With weather turning cold Dan asked Ollie for the old coat to give to a woman who did not own a coat. Ollie refused to part with the old coat so Dan went to the coat closet, took out the new coat and gave it away instead, stating one coat was all his wife needed to keep her warm during winter.

Following the 1947 high school graduation of their daughter Mary Ellen, Dan's retired from carpentry work in 1948. Soon after retiring Ollie and Dan purchased a 140-acre farm near the small rural community of Rossville in Lincoln County, Oklahoma. In 1950 the Rossville property was sold to buy a nearby farm located on the southwest corner of the Jacktown community. At the time of purchase the Jacktown community consisted of four gas stations, one at each corner of the intersection and a few houses dotted about the landscape. Neither farm was ever tilled, but they did accommodate a few head of cattle, a horse or two, and at times a couple of goats, a few dogs, and any stray cats that wandered in.

While living at the Jacktown location Dan was killed. Returning home from grocery shopping in preparation for Thanksgiving he made a left turn into his driveway and was broadsided by an oncoming automobile. The accident was in part attributed to misting rain creating diminished visibility and slick pavement. Initially it was thought he wasn't injured seriously, sustaining only a bump on the side of the head. While at the accident scene Dan collapsed and died from a blood clot that quickly formed in his temple. He was killed on Hwy 62 less than a quarter mile west of Jacktown.

Dan died on 22 Nov 1952. He is buried at Rossville Cemetery, Lincoln County, Oklahoma.

After the death of her husband, Ollie sold the Jacktown farm in 1953. Ollie and her mother Malisa who was residing with her in Jacktown returned to Oklahoma City and the home Dan and Ollie had owned prior to purchasing the farms.

In 1957 Ollie and her mother returned to Lincoln County. After purchasing a small corner section of the farm belonging to daughter Mary and son-in-law Leonard she built a home. The house was located southwest of the small rural community of Midlothian.

Ollie never learned to drive an automobile. Therefore she relied on her son-in-law to take her into town once a month to cash her social security check, pay bills, and purchase groceries.

After the death of her mother Malisa, Ollie spent much of her time with grandchildren. When they came to visit she would bake or cook their favorite food. Ollie enjoyed baking and often prepared sugar cookies for her grandchildren. When cooking and baking she never measured anything, but rather reached into the cabinet, pulled out what she needed, and then measured a portion into her hand, or else poured the ingredient directly into the bowl until she felt the amount was sufficient. Pancakes made from scratch were often prepared as a morning breakfast before sending a grandchild off to catch the school bus. Other breakfast offerings commonly included Kellogg's Corn Flakes and grapefruit halves. There was also fresh squeezed orange juice waiting on the breakfast table.

Each Sunday Ollie prepared a noontime dinner for her daughter's family. The meal preparations would be nearing completion by time Mary and her family returned from church service. Sunday dinners typically consisted of fried chicken, mashed potatoes with white cream gravy, green beans seasoned with bacon drippings, whole kernel or cream corn, a Jell-O salad, and for dessert it was either lemon or chocolate cream pie. As a change, a layered white coconut cake served as dessert. On occasion the Sunday meal menu changed from fried chicken to pot roast served with roasted potatoes, carrots, and onions, and brown gravy.

When a grandchild came to spend the night Ollie would have waiting their favorite dish. For Sharalyn it was stewed potatoes. For Steven she would sometimes prepare a chocolate pie. There were always cokes in the refrigerator and ice cream in the freezer for making coke floats. Rarely was the owl shaped cookie jar ever empty. When Ollie went grocery shopping, chocolate candy bars were specifically selected for each grandchild's preference.

When her grandchildren were young Ollie would entertain them with crafts. She would teach how to cut paper dolls from a newspaper, or make a kite from sticks, old newspapers, and clothe scrapes. Making sunbonnets was also a recreation. Not one to discard things needlessly, Ollie crochets scraps of fabric into throw rugs using wooden crochet needles hand carved by her late husband Dan. Old nylon hosiery was braided and stitched into small area rugs. Even though her eyesight was poor, she spent time embroidering designs on flour sacks later used as tea towels. Pillowcases were also purchased and decorated with stitching. With aid of a magnifying glass she spent evenings reading from her Bible.

Ollie was addicted to the soap opera *The Edge of Night*. Her monthly trip into town had to be planned around the program's afternoon airtime. She also enjoyed watching westerns aired during primetime TV. *Gunsmoke* and *Bonanza* were her favorites. They were also favorite shows of her son-in-law, Leonard. Each week they would watch the televised series together.

During gardening months Ollie tended her zinnia beds, using the bright floral blooms as bouquets to decorate her home.

During the mid-1960s Ollie's eyesight deteriorated to the point she was near blind. Seeking medical correction she had cataracts removed and then several years later underwent a cornea transplant.

By the early 1970s Ollie's mind began to decline. The summer of 1975 her hip gave way causing her to fall from a chair as she was reaching into the cabinet. During the tumble she broke a leg. After undergoing surgery to repair the break, she was placed into an elderly care facility. While residing there she shared a room with her sister Bessie. Not long after being admitted to the facility Ollie could no longer recognize or remember family members.

After the passing of Bessie, Ollie was relocated to a facility closer to family. It was in Stroud, Lincoln County, Oklahoma she passed away on 1 Mar 1980. She is buried next to her beloved Dan at Rossville Cemetery near Rossville in Lincoln County Oklahoma.

Ollie and Dan Stevens had the following children:
Mary Ellen Stevens

MARY ELLEN STEVENS was born on 21 Jul 1929 at St. Anthony's Hospital in Oklahoma City, Oklahoma County, Oklahoma. In childhood she was called Mary Ellen. It is possible she was named in honor of her Grandpa Gunter's sister, Mary Ellen Gunter.

Raised an only child, Mary was spoiled by a doting father. During depression times her family was faced with a medical emergency when Mary's appendix ruptured. Following immediate surgery she was confined to the hospital until fully recovered. While there her father purchased as a get well gift, a Princess Elizabeth doll that in reality the family could not afford. It was during this hospital confinement Mary developed a hatred for oranges. Thereafter she stated countless times how she disliked even the thought of an orange, adding the smell of one made her ill. The distaste was attributed to orange juice used to camouflage the horrid taste of the medicine she was forced into taking during her recovery.

Mary considered her Aunt Vida more so an older sister than an aunt. During Mary's childhood they often spent time doing things together. Mary talked about when the family resided near Choctaw Vida lived with them for a short duration. Another family member she was close to was her cousin Carl Miller, viewing him more as the brother she never had than as a cousin. Each an only child, when growing up they were often together. As adults the two made a point of getting together at the Stewart home in July. During the visit Carl and Leonard would sit on the front porch and churn homemade ice cream. The event was somewhat a family tradition.

As a child Mary loved visiting her grandfather Gunter's farm. The Gunter clan gathered often giving her numerous cousins with which to spend the day. During visits her grandfather often saddled up Old Alice for the kids to ride.

After the death of her grandfather Gunter, the Stevens family continued making trips to the Canute homestead. To entertain an afternoon Mary would flush out and chase jackrabbits around the prairie pasture with cousins Johnny Ray and George Wayne Gunter.

Mary attended Putman City Public School System for twelve years, graduating in May 1947. In her high school annual produced her senior year she is pictures as a member of The Twelve Year Club. Mary stated many times that her family moved often, sometimes several times a year but they always remained within the Putman City School District.

Trained in stenography and secretarial work, following high school graduation Mary sought clerical employment at Tinker Field Air Force Base in Midwest City. She held big dreams of becoming a career woman with thought of possibly moving to Alaska. If not Alaska, then she wanted to own a large cattle ranch in New Mexico.

When the Stevens family moved to Rossville Mary was forced into carpooling to and from her job at Tinker Field. Not owning a car and having no idea how to operate one, it left her dependent on other Tinker AFB employees living in the area. It was while commuting to work she met her future husband Leonard J. Stewart, also an employee of Tinker Field. Much to Mary's dissatisfaction Leonard had his eye on her and was set on making her his wife.

After getting to know Leonard and realizing they shared the same dream of owning a New Mexico cattle ranch Mary conceded to a partnership marriage. The marriage was planned to take place 1 Oct 1950. At the last minute she decided to back out of the agreement. With bags packed in preparation for heading to parts unknown Mary was on her way out the door headed for the nearest bus stop when Leonard suddenly appeared in her driveway several hours ahead of schedule. The marriage took place in Chandler, Lincoln County, Oklahoma on the afternoon of October 1st in the home of Reverend William Fox. Brother Fox was the pastor of Horton Chapel Church of the Nazarene located near the small community of Rossville. After the private ceremony the couple spent their honeymoon in Colorado Springs, Colorado. Jonathan Leonard Stewart (known as Leonard J. Stewart) was born 6 Feb 1924 in rural Scott County, Virginia, the son of Lucian Bell and Ella Mae (Williams) Stewart.

Leonard and Mary continued employment at Tinker AFB until after purchasing a 160-acre farm in 1952. The fertile bottom land was located along Kickapoo Creek, a small tributary of the Deep Fork of the North Canadian River that flowed near the small rural community of Midlothian in Lincoln County, Oklahoma. They soon purchased an additional 80 acre section of pastureland adjoining their original purchase. Quitting her position at Tinker AFB Mary settled into the life of a housewife and homemaker. While her husband spent his days in the fields plowing, planting, and harvesting crops, she spent her time in the garden planting, harvesting, and then canning the produce. Together they managed the farm and herd of Shorthorn dairy cattle.

Mary and Leonard purchased an additional farm in 1962. The property adjoined their original farm and offered a larger house for their expanding family. By this time the dairy cattle had transitioned into beef cattle requiring less daily attention thus allowing more time for farming.

Mary did not acquire a driver's license until after 1970. When her socially active children required both she and Leonard chauffeur kids in different directions to scheduled school events she was forced into obtaining a driver's license. Until then her driving had been limited to maneuvering the hay truck around the field while Leonard loaded and stacks bales for storing, and on occasion when she delivered noontime meals to hired hands working in the fields.

With onset of the 1970s, Leonard and Mary sought employment outside of farm life. For a while they both worked at the newly opened garment factory in Chandler, Oklahoma. Neither finding Denier Mills a satisfactory job they enrolled at Gordon Cooper Vocational-Technical School in Shawnee, Oklahoma where they attended evenings classes several times a week. Remaining in the clerical field Mary trained for data processing while Leonard learned the skill of welding. After completion of their respective course they sought employment in Oklahoma City. Leonard was hired as a welder at Robberson Steel Company located at 4th and Blackwelder and Mary found employment as a secretary at Agro Cattle Company located on NW 63rd Street.

Due to demands of farming and ranching Leonard sought employment closer to home. In 1976 he was hired at the newly opened Wolverine Tube Plant in Shawnee, Oklahoma. It was there he worked until his health deteriorated.

Considering divorce, Mary remained in the city. Acquiring an apartment near NW 63rd Street and May Avenue she walked to and from work five days a week.

In time Mary decided to return to Leonard and the farm. In Chandler she found employment as a file clerk at the Lincoln County Department of Social Services.

In the spring of 1978 Leonard was diagnosed with cancer. After a courageous battle he lost the fight on 25 Oct 1979. He is buried at Rossville Cemetery near Rossville in Lincoln County, Oklahoma.

Following her husband's death Mary remained on the farm and continued with employment at the Department of Human Service until suffering a stroke in early January 1990. The medical condition forced her into early retirement. Upon release from an extended stay at the hospital she spent several additional months in rehabilitation, making a remarkable recovery.

In the spring of 1991 Mary sold the livestock and all the farm equipment, and then rented the property for farming and pasture. In the spring of 1995 she placed for sale all but 100 acres of the farms known as Kickapoo Valley Farms. After completion of the sale she purchased a house in Shawnee, Oklahoma.

Mary resided at 6 Apache Street in Shawnee until 3 Feb 2005. On that date she left for a scheduled doctor's appointment and never returned home. That afternoon she was admitted into the hospital for test to determine the cause of her distress. She remained in the hospital for the most of two weeks before discharged. Too weak to care for herself, she was placed into an elderly care facility in Meeker, Oklahoma. The arrangement lasted less than a week. Mary insisted she was leaving with or without anyone's blessing or help. To appease her wishes, Mary's youngest daughter Robin moved her to Edmond, Oklahoma. It was agreed that Mary would live with her daughter and son-in-law until more agreeable arrangements could be made.

While residing in Edmond Mary was again admitted into the hospital. After an extended stay and an extensive battery of test it was diagnosed she was suffering from advanced cirrhosis of the liver. It was determined her liver was scared from possibly contracting meningitis when young and the condition going undiagnosed and untreated.

Mary Ellen Stevens-Stewart passed away 18 Jul 2005 in Edmond, Oklahoma County, Oklahoma. She is buried next to her parents, Daniel and Ollie Stevens at Rossville Cemetery near Rossville, Lincoln County, Oklahoma.

Mary and Leonard Stewart had the following children:
  A. Sharalyn Marie Stewart
  B. Steven Alan Stewart
  C. Robin Jeanette Stewart
  D. Scott Leonard Stewart

  A. Sharalyn Marie Stewart was born on 3 February 1955 in Chandler, Lincoln County, Oklahoma. She was the pride and joy of her father Leonard and quite the daddy's girl. Born three days shy of her father's birthday, life was spent combining the birthday celebrations.

Achieving school age, Sharalyn attended a rural grade school known as Springdale District #75. On the first day of school she boarded the bus with expectation of knowing how to read by time she returned home that evening. Having patience was never one of Sharalyn's attributes. She graduated 8th Grade from the rural country school in 1968 and from Chandler High School on 18 May 1973.

While employed as a cashier at a fast foods restaurant in Oklahoma City Sharalyn met Edwin Lynn Kerbo, known as Lynn. In 1975 they on 13 May in Oklahoma City, Oklahoma County, Oklahoma. Her brother Steven Stewart served as witness to the civil ceremony. Lynn was born in 1952 in Oklahoma, the son of Bernal Lee and Violet Christine (Allen) Kerbo. Sharalyn and Lynn divorced.

Sharalyn is a veteran of Desert Storm.

Sharalyn and Lynn Kerbo have the following children:
  KristiLynn Marie Kerbo

  KristiLynn Marie Kerbo, known as Kris or Kristi was born in 1976 in Oklahoma.
  KristiLynn married Andrew Louis Williams on 25 May 1997 in Lakeland, Polk County, Florida.
  The ceremony was officiated by his grandmother Kathleen Williams. Andy was born in 1974 in
  Florida, the son of Tommy and Marcia Lou (Wyman) Williams.
  Kristi and Andy enjoy fishing, hunting, watching movies and spending time with nieces and
  nephews.
  Kristi and Andy have no children.

  B. Steven Alan Stewart was born in 1956 in Oklahoma. He was nicknamed Stevie by his older sister Sharalyn.

Steven attended Springdale School for 8 years, graduating Salutatorian of his class in 1970. Continuing with his education he graduated from Chandler High School in May 1974.

Steven married Linda Lou Henderson on 4 Dec 1976 in Lincoln County, Oklahoma at Horton Chapel Church of the Nazarene located near Rossville. Linda was born in 1958 in Louisiana, the daughter of Robert and Cherie Henderson. Steve and Linda divorced.

Furthering his education, Steven graduated with a bachelor's degree from Bethany Nazarene College in Bethany, Oklahoma. He later achieved a master's degree in Geriatrics.

Steve and Linda Stewart had the following children:
    Amber Leigh Stewart

    Amber Leigh Stewart was born in 1981 in Oklahoma.
    Amber graduated Yukon High School in 2000. Continuing with her education she enrolled in Oklahoma City University, obtaining a Bachelor of Science degree in 2004, and a Master's Degree in Criminal Justice in 2006.
    Amber married her high school sweetheart Tyler Fankhauser on 28 Aug 2008 in Guthrie, Logan County, Oklahoma.
    Amber loves spending time with her daughter, shopping, arts and crafts, and scrapbooking.
    Amber and Tyler Fankhauser have the following children:
        Lindee Leigh Fankhauser

 C. Robin Jeanette Stewart was born in 1959 in Oklahoma. During childhood she was nickname Bobby Socks by her dad and called Jeannette by her Stewart aunts.

Robin attended her first eight years of school at Springdale. Following graduation she attended Chandler High School, graduating in May 1977.

The summer prior to graduation Robin attended classes at Oklahoma Baptist University in Shawnee, Oklahoma. It was there she met her future husband, Joseph Dickerson. Following high school graduation Robin attended Bethany Nazarene College in Bethany, Oklahoma.

Robin married Joseph William Dickerson on 29 Aug 1978 at Horton Chapel Church of the Nazarene near Rossville in Lincoln County, Oklahoma. Joseph (known as Joe) was born in 1957 in Oregon, the son of Lester Eugene and Edith Mae (O'Hara) Dickerson.

Robin enjoys spending free time traveling and entertaining her grandchildren.

Robin and Joseph Dickerson have the following children:
    Christina Rene Dickerson

    Christina Rene Dickerson (known as Chris) was born in 1979 in Oklahoma.
    Chris attended Oklahoma Baptist University (OBU) in Shawnee, Oklahoma.
    Christina married Anthony Eugene Stokes, Jr. (Tony) on 14 Dec 2002 in Oklahoma City, Oklahoma County, Oklahoma. Tony was born in 1978, the son of Anthony Eugene and Joy Stokes.
    Christina and Anthony Stokes, Jr. have the following children:
        Anthony Eugene Stokes III
        Samantha Casey Stokes

D. Scott Leonard Stewart was born in 1962 in Oklahoma. During childhood he was referred to as Scotty.

Scott attended Springdale grade school until its closure in 1976. He was then transferred to the Chandler Public School system. During his Junior year of high school he attended Markoma Bible Academy in Tahlequah, Oklahoma.

Scott studied at Gordon Cooper Vo-Tech in Shawnee, Oklahoma where he trained to be a Draftsman. Following completion of the course he was hired by Allen-Bradley Corporation in Shawnee. The industry later sold and become TDK.

Scott married Angela May Shimko on 17 Jun 1995 in Tulsa, Tulsa County, Oklahoma. Angela was born in 1974, the daughter of Rev. Joseph and Patricia May (Mackrill) Shimko. Their wedding ceremony was conducted by her father.

Scott and Angela Stewart have the following children:
1. Danielle Elizabeth Stewart
2. Britni Nicole Stewart
3. Johnathon Scott Stewart
4. Sydney Kate Stewart

1. Danielle Elizabeth Stewart was born in 1997 in Oklahoma. She attends Chandler Public School and Gordon Cooper Technology Center. She has represented Gordon Cooper Technology Center in national competition in her chosen career field of Engineering. She enjoys robotics, participating in sports, music, and church activities.
2. Britni Nicole Stewart was born in 1999 in Oklahoma. She attends Chandler Public School, actively participating in 4-H and FFA. Britni has a genuine love for all animals. In kindergarten her goal in life was to become a veterinarian. It remains her career goal. She enjoys arts and crafts, and reading.
3. Johnathon Scott Stewart, known as 'Little Scotty' or Scotty to his parents was born in 2002 in Oklahoma. He attends Chandler Public School. By age 4 he was a whiz kid at playing video games. He is a participant in 4-H and Boy Scouts, and enjoys playing basketball. Scotty is also active in his church youth group.
4. Sydney Kate Stewart was born in 2006 in Oklahoma. She attends Chandler Public School. Sydney has a passion for animals, exhibiting swine, poultry, and sometimes rabbits at the county fair. She loves to sing and dance and participates in dance classes. Her favorite type of dancing is ballet.

Bessie Lee Gunter

BESSIE LEE GUNTER was born 12 Mar 1897 near Homer, Chickasaw Nation Indian Territory (Oklahoma). In infancy her father relocated the family to H County, later to be named Wichita County. The family settled northeast of Burns. When the community of Canute came into being the homestead was located a few miles to the east. She grew up helping with daily chores and working the cotton patch on the family farm.

When Bessie was young she experienced a severe case of poison ivy. The rash got into her eyes, destroying eyesight and causing near blindness. Her education level was limited by her eyesight and the need of her assistance helping work the homestead. The 1940 US Census recorded her highest level of education completed as third grade.

In the mid 1920's Bessie left the Canute farm and moved to Oklahoma City, Oklahoma. In the 1927 US City Directory published for Oklahoma City, Oklahoma, Bessie Gunter can be found residing at 1733 Linwood Blvd employed as a maid. In the 1928 edition of the directory she is sharing a residence with sisters, Betty, Hattie, Ollie, and Nell at 624 W 7th Street. In the 1929 publication of the US Cities Directory for Oklahoma City, Bessie is listed as Mrs. Bessie L. Gunter residing at 710 N. Durland Avenue with sisters Betty, Hattie, Ollie, and Nell.

Living in the city Bessie met Alfred Chase Brown, a college educated man previously married twice. A copy of their marriage record states they applied for the license on 17 April 1930. The marriage was performed April 20th in Oklahoma City, Oklahoma County, Oklahoma. Bessie and Alfred were united by Carl Trant, Justice of the Peace. Alfred Chase or A. C. as he was known, was born 8 Apr 1893 in Smith Center, Kansas. He was the son of Howard and Amy M (Haney) Brown. At time of their meeting Alfred was employed as an Oklahoma City law enforcement officer.

Bessie and Alfred first purchased a lot with a small house at 1404 S. Robinson Street in Oklahoma City. Grandson Stephen Brown stated it was on this property Alfred built a welding shop and established a business. In the 1931-1933 US City Directory published for Oklahoma City, Oklahoma, Bessie L and

Alfred C Brown are residing at 1404 S. Robinson Street. Alfred continued employment as a policeman working for the City of Oklahoma City.

It was stated in conversation with Stephen Brown that Alfred ran for the office of Oklahoma County Sheriff but was defeated in the election.

By the 1934 publication of US City Directory published for Oklahoma City, Oklahoma, Bessie and Alfred have purchased another home and relocated their residence to 820 SW 31st Street. Alfred has quit the police force to operate an auto repair shop located at his previous residence, 1404 S. Robinson Avenue. In the 1936-1942 directories Alfred lists occupation as 'auto salvage' with his business located on Robinson Avenue.

In the 1940 US Census taken on April 13th Bessie states they own their home and gives it a value of $2300.00. She adds that Alfred works a 60-hour week as a proprietor, owning a repair shop where he worked fifty-two weeks during the year 1939.

Grandson Stephen Brown said that during WW II Alfred was briefly employed as a carpenter at Tinker Field AFB.

In the 1944 US City Directory published for Oklahoma City, Oklahoma, Bessie and Alfred's residence remains the same. Alfred lists his occupation as manager of Brown's Auto Salvage. In this publication, the business is listed separately as Brown's Auto Salvage located at 1404 S Robinson. In 1948-1951 directories Alfred lists his business as AC Brown Auto Repair.

The US City Directories for Oklahoma City, Oklahoma does not list again an occupation or business for Alfred until 1959. In this edition Alfred lists his business as Browns Custom Mufflers. The directory lists son Elmer E as manager for Browns Custom Mufflers.

In the mid-1960s Bessie's eyes developed cataracts. With hope of improving vision she underwent several operations for the removal of cataracts.

Alfred passed away on 24 Jun 1976 in Oklahoma City, Oklahoma County, Oklahoma. He is buried at Resthaven Memorial Gardens in Oklahoma City.

Bessie devoted her life to being a homemaker and mother. It was at the house on SW 31st Street she and Alfred raised their family. Like her older sisters Bessie never learned to operate an automobile.

Bessie passed away in Oklahoma City, Oklahoma County, Oklahoma on 30 Jun 1979. She is buried next to her husband Alfred at Resthaven Memorial Gardens in SW Oklahoma City.

Bessie and Alfred Brown had the following children:
  1. Alfred Lee Brown
  2. Elmer Ellsworth Brown
  3. Floyd Lester Brown

1. ALFRED LEE BROWN was born on 29 Oct 1930 in Oklahoma City, Oklahoma County, Oklahoma. Alfred Lee as he was known grew up assisting his father at the family owned salvage yard and welding shop. It was there he spent many hours watching and assisting his father.

Alfred Lee graduated from Capitol Hill High School around 1948.

Following graduation Alfred Lee enlisted in the US Army. Serving his enlistment he was honorably discharged.

In the 1955 US City Directory published for Oklahoma City, Oklahoma, Alfred Lee is residing at home with his parents while employed as a mechanic at Tinker AFB.

Alfred Lee married Anita R. (last name unknown). They divorced.

In the 1959 US City Directory for Oklahoma City, Oklahoma, Alfred Lee is indexed with wife Nita R, residing at 223 SE 43rd Street. He lists occupation as an electrician at Tinker AFB.

Alfred Lee and Anita Brown had the following children:
  Kendal Brown
  Dean Brown
  Shelly Brown

Alfred Lee married (wife unknown). They had one son:
  Billy Brown.

Alfred Lee Brown passed away 10 May 2009 in Las Vegan, Clark County, Nevada.

2. ELMER ELLSWORTH BROWN was born 25 May 1932 in Oklahoma City, Oklahoma County, Oklahoma. Like his older brother he grew up helping his father at the auto salvage yard and welding shop.

Elmer attended Capitol Hill High School graduating about 1950. It was noted by nephew Stephen Brown that Elmer attended college but quit before obtaining a degree, stating Elmer had a great aptitude for mathematics.

Elmer married Norma Jean Brown of Oklahoma City, Oklahoma on 1 Sep 1951. The union was officiated by Justice of the Peace R. C. Trammel in Oklahoma City, Oklahoma County, Oklahoma. Nothing is known of Miss Norma Jean Brown other than prior to marriage she resided at 630 SE 29th Street in Oklahoma City. The marriage license states she was 18 years of age at time of application.

In the 1952 US City Directory for Oklahoma City, Oklahoma Elmer E Brown is listed as a widower residing at the home of his parents.

Elmer was drafted into military service for the Korean Conflict. Before completing enlistment he was reported AWOL and discharged from service.

In the 1955 US City Directory published for Oklahoma City, Oklahoma, Elmer E Brown is residing at 812 SE 31st Street and gives occupation as a factory worker at Robberson Steel. The 1959 directory again lists Elmer residing at home and gives his occupation as manager for Browns Custom Mufflers.

Nephew Stephen Brown stated that Elmer was employed briefly at the Wonder Bread Bakery in Oklahoma City and worked for a year at Tinker AFB. Most his employment entailed working at his father's muffler shop as a skilled welder.

Elmer married Emma Mae Shockley. They divorced.

Elmer passed away 7 Mar 2013 in Muskogee, Muskogee County, Oklahoma. He is buried near Muskogee, Oklahoma next to his wife, Emma Mae.

Elmer and Emma Brown had the following children:
  Lonnie Brown
  Jerry Brown
  Teresa Brown

3. FLOYD LESTER BROWN was born on 10 Sep 1933 in Oklahoma City, Oklahoma County, Oklahoma. Following in his brothers footsteps Floyd spend a great deal of time at his father's welding shop. It was there he learned the skill of welding which he used throughout his life.

Floyd attended Capitol Hill High School, quitting his education during his 10th year.

Floyd was drafted into the US Army to serve during the Korean Conflict. During his enlistment he worked as a welder. After an honorable discharge from service Floyd sought employment at Tinker AFB. While working at Tinker AFB he transferred to the FAA.

Floyd was educated in electronics. While working fulltime at Tinker AFB, he was self-employed part-time from his home as an electrician, a mechanic, and a mechanical repairman for electrical appliances and refrigeration.

The 1959 US City Directory published for Oklahoma City, Oklahoma Floyd is listed as residing with his parents and employed as a warehouseman at Tinker AFB.

Floyd married Carol (last name unknown). They divorced.

Floyd married Patricia Lennel Beatty (known as Lennel) in Texas. They divorced.

Stephen Brown stated his father had a big heart and was always helping people by repairing their appliances, working on their automobile, or other acts of kindness. He added that his father once built a television set from a kit and when finished gave it away.

Floyd passed away on 3 Jun 2005 in Texas.

Floyd and Lennel Brown had the following children:
   A. Tammy Lennet Brown
   B. Randell Lane Brown
   C. Stephen Mark Brown
   D. Cheryl Ann Brown

   A. Tammy Lennet Brown was born in 1961 in Oklahoma. She marry Scott Stevens. They divorced.
      Tammy married Michael Mitchell. They divorced.
      Tammy married Marty Hinkle.
      Tammy has no children.
   B. Randall Lane Brown was born in 1962 in Oklahoma. He married Jerri Turner.
      They have the following children:
         i. Hanna Brown
         ii. Katie Brown
   C. Stephen Mark Brown was born in 1963 in Oklahoma. He married Lorie Hester. They divorced.
      Stephen and Lorie have the following children:
         i. Chase Brown
         ii. Tanner Lane Brown
,   iii. Jessica Classyn Brown
      Stephen married Robin Louise Thompson.
   D. Cheryl Ann Brown was born in 1965 in Oklahoma. She married Scott Pullium. They divorced.
      Cheryl and Scott Pullium have the following children:
         i. Chad Pullium
         ii. Brent Pullium
      Cheryl married Steven Parker.
      Cheryl and Steven Parker have the following children:
      Twin daughters:
         iii. Katlin Parker
         iv. Britney Parker

John Lester Gunter

JOHN LESTER GUNTER was born 31 Aug 1900 near Canute in Oklahoma Territory (Oklahoma). It was in this area he spent his childhood working on the family farm.

John attended school in Canute, completing four years of high school. After graduating he continued with his education, obtaining a degree from Barber's College.

In the 1910 US Census John is listed as Lester living with his parents, George and Malisa on Turkey Creek in Washita County, Oklahoma.

On ancestry.com/military records there is record of John registering for the WW I draft on 12 Sep 1918. He was residing in Washita County. The registration card offers the following information: *John Gunter residing at R.F.D. #1, Canute, Washita County, Oklahoma. Birth Date 30 Aug 1900. Age at time of registration is 18 years old. His present occupation is farming, employed by G.W. Gunter. Address of employer as well as nearest living relative are the same as John's given address. His physical description is given as medium in build, blue eyes and light brown hair. The card is dated 12 Sep 1918 by the Local Board of Washita County, Cordell, Oklahoma.*

Like his older brother Albert, John is missing from the 1920 US Census.

In the 1930 Federal Census John is residing on the home place near Turkey Creek with his parents, nieces, nephews and sister-in-law. Brother Albert is listed as head of household. John's marital status is stated as Single. His occupation is given as farmer.

John married Reba Avo Wilson about 1932 in Oklahoma. Reba (known as Avo) was born on 1 Aug 1907 in Waco, McLennan County, Texas. She was the daughter of George Rayford and Mamie Mae (Wood) Wilson. It is believed John and Avo lived near each other and that is how they met. Son George told a story entailing a time before his parents married stating that John and Avo would at times go turtle hunting together. Avo had a scar on one leg from an incident when she and John were hunting snapping turtles and the turtle latched onto her leg.

John spent a portion of his life living and working on the Gunter family farm near Canute that his father George settled in the late 1890s. In the early 1940s John purchased a farm near a small community in Oklahoma called Cat Town. It is said to have been located a few miles from Henrietta. John worked this farm until the death of his father, at which time he returned to Canute to assist his widowed mother maintain the family farm.

Jack Gunter stated he remembers childhood living on the Gunter homestead. Wood in that portion of Oklahoma was limited. Jack stated he spent may times collecting 'Prairie Chips' (dried manure) on the homestead to burn as fuel.

When John's mother Malisa decided to lease the farm and move to Oklahoma City, John purchased a farm near Chelsea in Rogers County, Oklahoma.

In 1955 John's wife Avo Gunter passed away on May 10th in Chelsea, Rogers County, Oklahoma. She is buried at the Chelsea Cemetery in Chelsea, Oklahoma.

Stated by daughter Janet "John continued to farm the Chelsea location until all but Norene and Jack had left home. He then moved into town and as his daughter Norene once put it 'he never put on a pair of overalls again'. Farming wasn't what he wanted to do but what was thrust upon him."

John passed away on 11 Nov 1978 in Chelsea, Rogers County, Oklahoma. He is buried next to his wife Avo at Chelsea Cemetery in Chelsea, Rogers County, Oklahoma.

John and Avo Gunter had the following children:
  1. Johnny Ray Gunter
  2. George Wayne Gunter
  3. Bonnie Ruth Gunter
  4. Infant Son Gunter
  5. Ida Norene Gunter
  6. Lillian Janet Gunter
  7. Jack Carroll Gunter
  8. Helen Elaine Gunter

   1. JOHNNY RAY GUNTER was born 3 Jun 1934 near Canute in Washita County, Oklahoma. He attended Canute Public School and later enlisted in the US Army.

Johnny Ray married Imogene Garvin, daughter of Albert B and Ruby Loraine (Paulson) Gunter. They wed on 17 Jun 1957 in Modesto, Stanislaus County, California. Wife Jeanne stated that not long afterwards Johnny was reassigned to a military installation in Pasco, Washington.

During Johnny's enlistment in the Army he served as a mailman and was assigned as a driver to officers, taking them wherever they needed to go. He in time requested and was granted a hardship discharge.

Johnny Ray relocated his family to Illinois. It was there he found employment at the J.I. Case Plant. At the factory he was assigned the position of putting belly pans onto tractors. His obituary states that he retired in 1989 after twenty years employment with the corporation.

Johnny passed away 13 Mar 2007 in Silvis, Rock Island County, Illinois. He is buried at the Rock Island National Cemetery in Rock Island, Rock Island County, Illinois.

Johnny Ray and his wife Jeanne were very involved with their church.

Johnny Ray and Imogene Gunter had the following children:
  Johnny Ray Gunter, Jr.
  Jonathan Gunter

2. GEORGE WAYNE GUNTER was born in 1935 in Oklahoma. He attended Canute Public School until the family relocated to the Chelsea area.

George enlisted in the US Army and spent a tour of duty stationed in Germany.

With exception of the few years his father owned a farm near Henrietta, George spent most of childhood growing up in the Canute area. Living not far from the town of Canute, George and his brother Johnny walked to and from school. George told the story of one day when he and Johnny were walking home they saw a man lying dead in a field belonging to the family. It was later rumored the man had been killed by the Mafia and dumped in the pasture.

Another time when he and brother Johnny were walking home from school they discovered an overturned car in a ditch. Investigating the accident they found beer containers scattered around the crash site and the occupants of the car dead. They rushed home to tell their mother who gave them a difficult time with their story before believing them.

Yet another story told by George was that one day his father John was driving down the road running alongside the family farm and crashed the car into the bridge built over the small creek cutting across the road. George stated he had some good times and good memories of living on the farm.

George married Darlene Speir of Chelsea, Roger's County, Oklahoma.

George and Darlene lived in Illinois where George was employed by John Deere Manufacturing Company.

After retirement George and Darlene settled on an acreage in Wisconsin. It was on this property George worked several years building his house and surrounding outbuildings.

George's brother Jack stated he and George at one time had a gold claim in California. When their busy lives allowed getaway time they would spend at least 30 days each trip panning and mining for gold. Jack stated it was an enjoyable hobby and they usually found enough gold flakes to cover the expense of their trip.

George and Darlene Gunter had the following children:
  Debbie Gunter
  Howard Gunter
  Neil Gunter

3. BONNIE RUTH GUNTER was born on 11 Apr 1937 in Sentinel, Washita County, Oklahoma.

Bonnie married Randolph Tripp of Canute, Washita County, Oklahoma. They divorced.

The US City Directory published in 1969 for the City of Shafter, California has record of Bonnie and Randolph Tripp residing at 2318 Sycamore Drive. Randolph employed at Verl-Frost.

Bonnie and Randolph Tripp had the following children:
  Randolph Wade Tripp
  Sherrie L Tripp
  Shelli L Tripp (1965-1965)

Bonnie married Morris DeWitt Rushing on 25 Jul 1981 in Calaveras, California. Norris was born 17 Oct 1927 in Port Gibson, Mississippi, the son of Douglas and Margrite C (King) Rushing.

In the US Phone and Address Directory, 1993-2002, Bonnie and Morris Rushing are listed as residing at 3316 Aslin Street in Bakersfield, California from 1997-2002.

Morris passed away on 5 May 2005 in Bakersfield, Kern County, California.

Bonnie passed away on 23 Jan 2012 in California.

Bonnie and Morris Rushing had no children.

4. BABY GUNTER (1939-1939) unnamed son of John and Avo Gunter was born near Canute in Washita County, Oklahoma. Interment is at a Page Cemetery in Washita County, Oklahoma.

5. IDA NORENE GUNTER known as Norene was born in 1940 in Oklahoma.

Norene married William Warren Huffman (known as Billy) on 21 May 1960 in Chelsea, Rogers County, Oklahoma. They divorced.

Norene and Billy Huffman had the following children:
  Rusty Huffman
  Charlie Huffman
  Gary Huffman
  David Huffman

6. LILLIAN JANET GUNTER, known as Jan was born in 1942 in Oklahoma.

Janet married Jerry Ray Reed on 22 May 1959 in Chelsea, Rogers County, Oklahoma. Jerry was born in 1937 in Oklahoma, the son of Ray and Dolly Reed. Janet and Jerry divorced.

Janet and Jerry Reed had the following children:
  A. LaDonna Elaine Reed
  B. Jerry Allen Reed

Janet married Cornelius K Palmer (known as Lucky) in Sep 1966 at Cocoa Beach, Florida. Lucky was born 4 Aug 1926 in Roanoke, Bedford County, Virginia, the son of Harry and Sarah (Fritz) Palmer. Cornelius died 27 Aug 2008 in Gainesville, Hall County, Georgia.

Janet and Cornelius Palmer had the following children:
  C. Stephanie Michelle Palmer
  D. David Blaine Palmer

Janet married Richard Dean Moulton on 31 Jul 1976 in Seattle, King County, Washington. Richard was born on 4 Jul 1926 in Walla Walla, Walla Walla County, Washington, the son of George and Anne (Chictchester) Moulton. Janet and Richard divorced. They had no children.

Following her divorce from Richard Moulton, Lillian legally changed her name to Janet Gunter. Janet enjoys spending time working on her hobbies, needlepoint and quilting.

  A. LaDonna Elaine Reed was born in 1960 in Florida. She married Rodney James Bailey on
     19 Dec 1981 in the state of Washington. Rodney was born in 1950 in Wichita, Sedgwick
     County, Kansas, the son of Robert Louis and Oleta LaVerne (Culton) Bailey.
     LaDonna and Rodney Bailey had the following children:
        Alexander James Bailey.
  B. Jerry Allen Reed was born in 1961 in Florida. He married Laura Unknown. They divorced.
     Jerry and Laura Reed had the following children:
        Bradley Allen Reed
     Jerry married Lori (last name unknown). She passed away.
     Jerry and Lori Reed had the following children:
        Jerry Allen Reed, Jr.
  C. Stephanie Michelle Palmer was born in 1966 in Florida. She married Loren Scott Adams.
     Loren was born in 1964 in Washington, State. They divorced.
     Stephanie and Loren Adams had the following children:
        Tasha Maree Adams
        Austin Blaine Adams
  D. David Blaine Palmer was born in1967 in Florida. He married Lisa Beth Dodson known as
     Beth. They divorced.

     David and Beth Palmer had the following children:
        Maigon Joan Palmer
        David John Richard Palmer

7. JACK CARROLL GUNTER was born in 1944 in Oklahoma. Nicknamed Jackie, he spent childhood growing up on his father's farm near Chelsea, Oklahoma. Jack talks about farm life and the family living in a small house with the only wintertime heat source being the wood stove his mother used for cooking. He also speaks of how good the meals were his mother prepared on the old stove and is amazed how she managed doing it.

Jack first attended a small one room rural school where all eight grades were house in the same building. He stated that in the 3rd grade he was the only student in his class.

After graduating 8th Grade from the rural school, Jack attended a year and a half at Chelsea High School. Quitting his sophomore year Jack later relocated to Florida to live with his sister Janet. On his 17th birthday he lied about his age to enlist in the US Army. Jack enlisted in Miami, Florida choosing Light Weight Infantry as his military occupation. He was then sent to Ft. Benning, Georgia.

In 1962 Jack was stationed in Korea along the DMZ and later assigned to a military post in Alaska. He was one of the first members trained for special duty as a Green Beret. Training for Special Forces was first at Ft. Bragg and then in Okanawa before assigned to duty in Viet Nam. During his military enlistments (1961-1969) he also trained as a Path Finder, his skill and training used to search out and set up landing areas behind enemy lines for US forces serving in Viet Nam. Jack also attended Jump School and Ranger Training, as well as a Jungle Training course.

Jack completed three 6-month tours of duty in Viet Nam, starting in 1965, stating he was just about everywhere in Viet Nam, from Chu Che to the Delta, to the Black Virgan Mt. In 1969 he was severely wounded while carrying out a mission. Damage to his left leg and arm inhibited his passing the physical examine required for reenlisted. At age 24, he was promoted to SFC E7 in April 1969 and in July the same year honorably discharged from service at Ft. Dix, New Jersey.

Jackie married Elizabeth Ann Fry on 4 Oct 1969 in Chelsea, Rogers County, Oklahoma. They divorced.

Jack worked a variety of occupations at various locations across the US. He was a welder by trade before settling on a career in the medical field. In Bettendorf, Iowa he was employed at the JI Case Manufacturing Plant as a welder. In Houston, Texas he worked off shore as a welder for Brown and Root, Western Hemisphere Region.

In Oklahoma Jack attended Emergency Medical Technician school in 1990 and 1991 for training to become a certified EMT. Passing the examine he served in the capacity of responding to medical emergencies. Jack went on to obtain certification as a paramedic. As a paramedic he was assigned duty on an ambulance until 1996. Remaining in the medical field he sought employment at Wagoner Community Hospital as an ER and ICU technician. The hospital offered to assist with his go to nursing school. Deciding to further his career and interest in the medical profession he accepted the offer.

At age 55, Jack graduated from Rogers State University in 1999, passing certification and becoming a Registered Nurse. He was then employed as an RN specializing as a chemo nurse at Tulsa Regional Medical Center. He worked at Tulsa Medical Center until one snowy day he was driving home from his shift on a slick icy road. It was during the traitorous trip he decided it was time to retire. Upon safely arriving home Jack called his employer to notify he would not be returning to work. Jacked retired in April 2009.

Jack has served as part of a medical team on multiple mission trips to remote villages in the Philippines.

Since retiring Jack enjoys spending time working around his acreage, cruising in his Corvette, building birdhouses in his workshop, and outdoor grilling. He also loves time spent with his grandchildren, and his three dogs.

Jack and Elizabeth Gunter had the following children:
  Conrad Gunter
  Valerie Gunter

8. HELEN ELAINE GUNTER was born 27 Jul 1947 near Canute in Washita County, Oklahoma.

A few years after the death of her mother Helen was enrolled at the Enid State School in Enid, Oklahoma. It was there she resided until the institution's closure.

Helen was a quiet girl with short dark hair and a lovely smile.

Helen passed away 10 Feb 2002 in Nowata, Nowata County, Oklahoma. She is buried at Chelsea in Rogers County, Oklahoma.

Helen never married.

Betty Jane Gunter

BETTY JANE GUNTER was born near Canute in Washita County, Oklahoma Territory on 6 Feb 1904. Riding in a wagon to and from school she attended classes at Canute Public Schools. The 1940 Census records her highest level of education completed was three years high school.

Betty moved from the Canute farm to Oklahoma City, securing employment as a bookkeeper in a dry goods store. In the 1926 edition of the US City Directory published for Oklahoma City, Oklahoma Betty lists as rooming at 417 N Harvey. She is employed as a clerk at Rorabaugh-Brown Dry Goods Company. In the 1927 directory she has moved to 710 N Durland Ave, Oklahoma City and continues employment at Rorabaugh-Brown Dry Goods Company working in the office. In 1928 her employment remains the same but she has relocated residency, the move taking her to 624 W 7th Street. She is listed living with sisters Hattie, Bessie, Nell, and Ollie. In 1929 Betty has returned to 710 N Durland Avenue in Oklahoma City and is residing with sisters Hattie, Bessie, and Nell.

In the 1930 US Census Betty, along with sister Hattie is listed as a lodger. They are residing at the residence of Amy M Lewis located at 300 NE 10th Street in Oklahoma City.

Niece Mary Ellen Stevens-Stewart remarked after Betty and Hattie relocated to the city they became to a degree Flappers of the 1920s. They were modern girls who enjoyed dancing, learned to drive, lived independently on their own, and found employment in the job market rather than remain and work at home until married.

Betty met Alvin Oliver Miller from Geary, Oklahoma. Alvin was born 12 Oct 1905 in Geary, the son of Dr. Emil E and Helena Marie (Albrecht) Miller. Betty and Alvin applied for a marriage license 11 Oct 1930 in Geary, Blaine County, Oklahoma and were married on Alvin's birthday, 12 Oct 1930. The ceremony was performed by N. Ferd Engle, minister of the Christian Church in Geary. Blaine County Marriage Records show sister Hattie married Alvin's twin brother Clarence on the same day at the same location. On the marriage license Betty states her residence as Geary, Oklahoma. [vi]

After the weddings Betty and sister Hattie along with their husbands share a house in Geary until the late 1930s. On occasion it was the gathering place for the Gunter family to celebrate holidays. There are family group photos taken in 1936 of both the Gunter and Miller families during a holiday celebration at Betty and Hattie's home in Geary.

The 1940 US Census gives record of Betty and husband Alvin living with sister Hattie and her husband Clarence in Geary, Oklahoma in 1935.

The 1939 US City Directory published for Oklahoma City, Oklahoma shows Betty and Hattie have returned to Oklahoma City. Betty and her husband Alvin and Hattie with her husband Clarence are residing at 222 SE 43rd Street. Alvin lists his occupation as laborer and Betty lists her occupation as a clerk employed at Halliburton's Department Store located at 327 W. Main Street.

In the 1940 US Census Betty and Alvin with son Carl continue to share a residence with Hattie and her husband Clarence. The families are residing at 222 SE 43rd Street in Oklahoma City. Betty is employed as an addressograph. (A person who uses an addressograph machine to stamp addresses.) The census reports Betty's income for 1939 as $780.00 and states she works 48 hours per week. Husband Alvin was unemployed and reported a yearly income of $48.00 while employed as a pumper for a paving company.

The US City Directory published for Oklahoma City in 1940 lists Betty and Alvin residing at the 43rd Street address, Alvin listing his occupation as a laborer. Betty continues her position at Halliburton's Department Store.

The 1941 US City Directory published for Oklahoma City, Oklahoma indicates Betty and Alvin with son Carl have relocated to a home of their own. They are residing at 218 SE 43rd Street. Alvin lists occupation as laborer and Betty continues employment as a clerk at Halliburton's Department Store. The same is stated in the 1942 City Directory.

Betty and Alvin are not found again in the US City Directory until 1945. They have returned to the 222 SE 43rd Street address in Oklahoma City where sister Hattie is on record as living the previous year. Betty is employed at OCAD (possibly stands for Oklahoma City or Oklahoma County Accounts Department). No occupation is listed for Alvin.

There is no city directory found for 1946. In 1947 Betty J and Alvin O are found in the directory residing at 222 SE 43rd Street in Oklahoma City. Alvin lists occupation as painter with no employment given for Betty. In the 1948 directory their address remains the same with no occupation stated.

The 1949 US City Directory published for Oklahoma City, Oklahoma states Betty J and Alvin O are residing at 222 SE 43rd Street. A separate listing for Mrs. Betty J Miller lists Betty employed as an office secretary at Carpenters and Joiners Local Union #329. In the 1951 directory Alvin O Miller lists his employment as an 'egg candler'. In the 1954 directory their address remains the same. In this edition Alvin lists his occupation as a driver.

Betty was employed as a secretary by Tinker AFB in Midwest City. It was from Tinker Field she retired as a civil service employee.

Betty passed away 15 Jul 1980 in Oklahoma City, Oklahoma County, Oklahoma. She is buried at Sunny Lane Cemetery in Del City, Oklahoma.

Alvin passed away 6 Aug 1986 in Oklahoma City, Oklahoma County, Oklahoma. He is buried at Sunny Lane Cemetery in Del City, Oklahoma.

Betty and Alvin Miller had the following children:
Carl Alvin Miller

CARL ALVIN MILLER, son of Betty Jane and Alvin Oliver Miller was born 20 Oct 1931 in Oklahoma. He began his education at Geary Public Schools. When his parents relocated to Oklahoma City he attended Oklahoma City Public Schools.

Both an only child, Carl and his cousin Mary Ellen Stevens were close companions while growing up in Oklahoma City. In later years Carl was a large man with a jolly personality.

Carl married Ruth Marie Knisek. They applied for a marriage certificate on 23 Dec 1950 in Oklahoma City, Oklahoma County, Oklahoma. Ruth was born on 6 Mar 1929 in Oklahoma, the daughter of Jarsolar William and Oma Knizek. Jarsolar William Knizek was a native of Czechoslovakia. His wife Oma was born in Oklahoma. Carl and Ruth divorced.

In the 1951 US City Directory published for Oklahoma City, Oklahoma Carl and Ruth are residing at 309 SE 41st Street. In the 1952 directory Carl and wife Ruth have no given address listed but it states Carl is employed as a deliveryman for Osler Prescription Shoppe.

The 1954 US City Directory published for Oklahoma City, Oklahoma lists Carl and wife Ruth residing at 1513 NE 16th Street. No occupation is listed.

The 1955 US City Directory published for Oklahoma City, Oklahoma gives record of Carl A Miller with wife Ruth residing at 1538 S Indiana Avenue. Carl lists employment as a driver for Capitol Hill Taxi. It was with Capitol Hill Taxi Service Carl was employed as a taxicab driver for many years, usually working the graveyard shift.

The 1959 US City Directory published for Oklahoma City, Oklahoma lists Ruth as Mrs. Ruth Miller residing at 2111 NW 33rd Street. She is employed as an office secretary at Tinker AFB. There is no listing found for Carl.

Carl was employed as a cab driver in Oklahoma City and as a security guard. Tonya Gunter stated she remembered him working as an Oklahoma City police officer.

Carl passed away on 10 Jun 1986 in Oklahoma City, Oklahoma County, Oklahoma. He is buried at Arlington Cemetery in Oklahoma City.

Carl and Ruth Miller had the following children:
A. Mary Wilhoma Miller
B. Paul Victor Miller

A. Mary Wilhoma Miller as born in 1954 in Oklahoma. She grew up caring for her twin brother Paul. Mary married David T Hutchison on 12 Nov 1971 in Cooke County, Texas. They divorced. Mary and David Hutchison the following children:
   Thomas Scott Hutchison
B. Paul Victory Miller was born in 1954 in Oklahoma. He never married.

Hattie Ellen Gunter

HATTIE ELLEN GUNTER was born near Canute in Oklahoma Territory on 7 Aug 1904. While attending school at Canute she road to class and back in a horse drawn wagon. Hattie helped work the family's cotton fields and assisted with household chores.

Hattie graduated from Canute High School before moving to Oklahoma City.

In the 1925 US City Directory published for Oklahoma City, Oklahoma, Hattie is rooming at 301 W 7th Street. She lists employment as a stenographer at Harris-Goar Company, a retailer in watches, diamonds, jewelry, and clothing. The establishment is located at 16-18 N Harvey Avenue. Hattie is the first of the Gunter girls to appear on record living in Oklahoma City.

In the 1926 US City Directory published for Oklahoma City, Oklahoma, Hattie with sister Betty are rooming at 417 N. Harvey. The directory indicates she remains employed at Harris-Goar Company as a stenographer. In 1927 she with sister Betty relocate their residence to 710 N Durland Avenue. In 1928 she with sisters Betty, Ollie, Bessie, and Nell are living at 624 W 7th Street. In 1929 she and her sisters return to the 710 N Durland Avenue address. Hattie remains employed as a stenographer for Harris-Goar Company.

The 1930 US City Directory published for Oklahoma City, Oklahoma records Hattie as residing at 129 E 12th Street, listing employment as a stenographer for VV Harris. In the same directory there is a Vernon V Harris Investments that may or may not be affiliated with Harris-Goar Company.

In the 1930 US Census Hattie with sister Betty are recorded as lodgers at the home of Amy M Lewis located at 300 NE 10th Street in Oklahoma City.

Hattie met Clarence E Miller, a twin brother to sister Betty's boyfriend Alvin O Miller. Hattie and Clarence applied for a marriage license on 11 Oct 1930 in Geary, Blaine County, Oklahoma. They were married the next day at the Christian Church in Geary. Clarence was the son of Dr. Emil E and Helena Marie (Albrecht) Miller. On the marriage license Hattie states her residence as Canute, Oklahoma. [vii]

After marriage Hattie with husband Clarence shared a home in Geary, Oklahoma with her sister Betty and brother-in-law Alvin.

In the US City Directory published for Oklahoma City, Oklahoma in 1937 and 1938 Hattie is again residing in Oklahoma City. The directories list her as Mrs. Hattie Miller living at 434 NW 6th Street. Occupation is listed as stenographer. There is no listing found for husband Clarence or sister Betty in either of these directories.

In the 1939 US City Directory published for Oklahoma City, Oklahoma Clarence E Miller is listed as residing with Hattie and they are living at 222 SE 43rd Street. Clarence lists occupation as laborer and Hattie gives employment as a stenographer at the County Department of Public Assistance. Sister Betty with husband Alvin are living at the same address.

The 1940 Census gives record of Hattie and Clarence residing at 222 SE 43rd Street in Oklahoma City. The census lists Clarence as head of household. The household consists of his wife Hattie, his brother Alvin, sister-in-law Betty and nephew Carl. Hattie is recorded as being employed the previous fifty-two weeks, working a forty-eight hour week as a stenographer for the State, giving her income for 1939 as $800.00. Clarence and his brother Alvin are unemployed and seeking work. It is recorded they each worked fourteen weeks during the year 1939, both employed as a pumper for a paving company.

The 1941 US City Directory published for Oklahoma City, Oklahoma lists Hattie and Clarence E Miller as residing at 222 SE 43rd Street. Clarence lists occupation as laborer. Hattie remains employed as a typist for the County Department of Public Assistance.

Clarence enlisted in the US Army 24 Aug 1942 in Tulsa, Tulsa County, Oklahoma. Clarence is a WW II veteran.

Hattie is not listed in the 1942 US City Directory published for Oklahoma City, Oklahoma and there is no 1943 directory for the area. It could be she and Clarence were living in the Tulsa area near his mother and it would explain his induction into service taking place in Tulsa.

In the 1944 US City Directory published for Oklahoma City, Oklahoma, Mrs. Hattie Miller is listed as residing at 222 SE 43rd Street. She is as an employee for Douglas Aircraft Company. This is the last Oklahoma City Directory found online at ancestry.com with Hattie living in Oklahoma City.

At some time after leaving Oklahoma City, Hattie and Clarence purchased a house on Place Street in Tulsa, Oklahoma. In Tulsa Clarence worked from home as a door-to-door sales representative for Watkins and Rawleigh Products. The commission from sales along with his investments in the stock market helped supplement the family income. In Tulsa Hattie was employment as a secretary for criminal cases at the District Attorney's Office.

After Hattie retired in the early 1970s, she and Clarence purchased a small acreage near Colcord, Oklahoma. They both loved fishing and Clarence had a reputation for catching fish from a pond or river when no one else could manage so much as a nibble on their hook. His favorite bait was blood bait or 'stink bait' as he called it. He had his own secret concoction that rarely failed to attract a 'whopper'. After purchasing the Colcord acreage Clarence had built a small pond and stocked it with bass and catfish he enjoyed feeding daily.

When not feeding his fish, Clarence was working in his organic garden where he had a large plot designated for raising plump red strawberries. Remainder of the garden grew a variety of vegetables which Hattie spent her time preserving. One of the first things he began after moving to the rural home was a compost pile to supply his organic garden. Clarence loved explaining the process of creating compost from discarded food, clean wheat straw and grass clippings, and the health benefits of eating organically raised produce. Talking about it brought a twinkle to his eyes and a smile to his face.

Hattie and Clarence drove a white Plymouth car. Rather than having a conventional transmission that shifted from the column, it was equipped with push buttons on the dashboard offering a selection of reverse, drive, neutral, and park.

Clarence passed away on 20 Sep 1986 in Colcord, Delaware County, Oklahoma. He is buried at the Row Cemetery in Colcord.

After the death of her husband Hattie sold the acreage and moved to Lamar, Colorado to live nearer her sister Vida Mae Sanderson. In Lamar Hattie lived independently until her health deteriorated and she could no longer care for herself.

Hattie passed away in Lamar, Prowers County, Colorado on 1 July 2002. She is buried at Row Cemetery in Colcord, Delaware County, Oklahoma.

Hattie and Clarence Miller had no children.

Nellie Gunter

NELLIE GUNTER (known as Nell) was born 29 Dec 1905 near Canute in Oklahoma Territory.[2] Nellie grew up assisting on the family farm and helping with housework.

Nell acquired her education at Canute, completing the first two years of high school. (1940 US Census)

Nell can be found in both the 1910 and 1920 US Census living with her parents and siblings on Turkey Creek in Washita County, Oklahoma.

Like her older sisters, Nell left the farm and moved to Oklahoma City. In 1927 the US City Directory published for Oklahoma City, Oklahoma records Nell Gunter residing at 523 N Dewey Avenue. In 1928 she is living with her sisters at 624 W 7th Street. She lists employment as a stenographer for JJ Milan (Real Estate Company). In 1929 Nell remains employed as a stenographer at JJ Milan and has relocated with her sisters to 710 N Durland Avenue.

Living in Oklahoma City Nell met Earlon Titus, a widower. A copy of the marriage license states Nell and Earl Lee Titus applied for a marriage license 9 Feb 1929, and on the same date were married by Judge George W. Clark in Oklahoma City, Oklahoma County, Oklahoma. Earlon Lee Titus was born on 6 May 1898 in Kentucky, the son of Charles Wesley and Minnie Ellen (Stucker) Titus.

In the 1930 US Census Nell is living at 1100 E 35th in Oklahoma City with husband Earl, and stepchildren Charles Wesley Titus and Johnny Mae Titus. The census states they own their home valued at $1000.00. They also own a radio. Age at first marriage for Earl is stated as 19 years old, Nell was 22 years old at time of her first marriage. Earl works in the housing industry, his occupation given as plasterer. The census states Earl is not a veteran.

---

[2] Nell's social security death index card gives birthdate as 29 Dec 1904. Hattie was born in Aug 1904. Nell's headstone gives the birth year as 1905. Nell's social security card was issued from the state of Oregon prior to 1951.

The 1930-1934 US City Directories published for Oklahoma City, Oklahoma gives record of Nell residing with husband Earl at 1029 E 35th Street. Earl lists his occupation as a plasterer.

In the 1935 US City Directory published for Oklahoma City, Oklahoma, Nell and Earl continue to reside at 1029 NE 34th Street. Earl lists his occupation as mechanic.

In the 1936 edition of the US City Directory published for Oklahoma City, Oklahoma, Nell and Earl are residing at 342 SE 38th Street. Earl lists his occupation as oil field worker.

There is no listing found for Nell or Earl in the 1937 edition of the directory. In 1938 they have returned to their address at 1029 NE 34th Street. Earl has resumed his occupation of plasterer.

In the 1940 US Census Nell and Earl are residing in Oklahoma City at their home on NE 34th Street. Included in the household are children Johnnie May, Charles Wesley, Jerry Lee and Aileen Gay. The given value of the home is $1000.00 and it is stated they own the residence. Earl is recorded as a private contractor specializing as a plasterer. He worked twelve hours during the week prior to the census. His income for 1939 was reported as $1450.00.

In the 1941 US City Directory published for Oklahoma City, Oklahoma, Nell and Earl are residing at their home on NE 34th Street. Earl is working as a plasterer. In 1942 the residence remains the same but Earl's occupation has changed to asbestos worker. The 1942 directory is the last published Oklahoma City directory listing Nell and Earl living in Oklahoma City.

By the mid-1950s Nell and her family have relocated to Midwest City, Oklahoma. Son Jerry Lee and daughter Aileen Gay are included in a Midwest City school yearbook published in 1954.

In April 1962 Earl passed away in Oklahoma City, Oklahoma County, Oklahoma. He is buried in Arlington Cemetery, Oklahoma City.

In the 1987 US Public Records Index found online at ancestry.com Nell is recorded as residing at 512 N Douglas Blvd in Oklahoma City. Her home was located off Douglas Blvd on an acreage near the city limits of Midwest City.

Nell passed away on 18 Jul 1991 in Newalla, Oklahoma County, Oklahoma. She is buried at Arlington Cemetery in Oklahoma City.

Nell and Earl Titus had the following children:
   A. Jerry Lee Titus
   B. Aileen Gay Titus

   A. JERRY LEE TITUS was born on 8 Apr 1932 in Oklahoma City, Oklahoma County, Oklahoma.

Jerry Lee attended Midwest City Public Schools.

Jerry enlisted in the US Army on 13 May 1946 in Oklahoma City, Oklahoma County, Oklahoma. He was discharged from service on 4 Aug 1952.

Jerry is listed in the US City Directory living in Midwest City in 1954. Also he is attending Midwest City High School. His class photo is published in the in the 1954 edition of the school's yearbook *The Bomber*. He is listed as a sophomore.

Military records found at ancestry.com show that in 1957 Jerry again enlisted in military service, this time opting for the US Navy. He entered service on 5 Dec 1957 and made the Navy his career. He retired 20 Sep 1974 with the identifying rank of AC-2.

Upon retirement Jerry settled in Hawaii. He is recorded in the US Phone and Address Directory (1993-2002) as living in Kapolei 1999-2002. (ancestry.com)

Jerry married Evelyn Y.A. Kim. Evelyn was born on 2 Feb 1921 and passed away 27 Sep 2003. She is buried at the Hawaii State Veterans Cemetery in Hawaii, Section 99-H Site 4.

Jerry passed away 20 Oct 2002 in Kapolei, Honolulu Hawaii. He is buried at the Hawaii State Veterans Cemetery in Hawaii, Section 99-H Site 4.

Jerry L Titus had the following children:
    Jerry W Titus

  B. AILEEN GAY TITUS was born 9 Mar 1938 in Oklahoma City, Oklahoma County, Oklahoma.

Aileen attended Midwest City High School, graduating the class of 1957. A sophomore photo of her is in a 1955 edition of the schools yearbook, *The Bomber*. (ancestry.com)

Aileen married Charles Neer Hannah. Charles was born on 21 Sep 1939 in Arkansas, the son of Fred Cono and Martha Ann 'Merl' (Jenkins) Hanna.

The US City Directory on ancestry.com lists Aileen G. Hanna living in Oklahoma City in 1977.

Aileen's husband Charles passed on away 6 Jan 1990 in Newalla, Oklahoma County, Oklahoma.

Aileen and Charles Hanna had the following children:
    Charlene Hanna
    Freddie Hanna
    Lori Hanna
    David Hanna

On ancestry.com, a 1991 US Public Records Index lists Aileen G Hanna residing in Lone Wolf, Oklahoma.

Aileen married (unknown) Blaylock in Altus, Oklahoma in 1992.

In the 1993 publication of the US Directories Aileen Blaylock is listed as living at 112 White Turkey Drive in Newalla, Oklahoma.

In a 1996 edition of US Phone and Address Directory Aileen Hanna is residing at 1320 McGregor Drive in Oklahoma City, Oklahoma. The directory references Aileen living at 112 White Turkey Drive in Newalla, Oklahoma in 1995 and residing in Lone Wolf, Oklahoma in 1991.

In the 2002 publication of US Directories, Aileen is residing at 112 White Turkey Drive under the name Aileen Blaylock. The address is given as Norman, Oklahoma rather than Newalla.

Aileen passed away on 22 Aug 2006 in Del City, Oklahoma County, Oklahoma. Social Security Death Index records found online at ancestry.com lists her as Aileen Blaylock. In her obituary published 25 Aug 2006 in the Daily Oklahoman she is named as Aileen Hanna. It gives mention of 15 grandchildren and 18 great-grandchildren.

Vida Mae Gunter

VIDA MAE GUNTER was born on 8 November 1915 near Canute, Washita County, Oklahoma. After moving with her parents to a ranch north of Canute her father George purchased a horse for Vida to ride to school and back. The horse was known as Old Alice. Old Alice was Vida's mode of transportation to class until she graduated Canute High School in 1934.

A statement once made by her sister Ollie was that Vida grew up never having to get her hands dirty. According to Ollie, unlike rest of the Gunter children Vida never knew what it was to labor long hours under a hot sun working in the cotton field.

Following graduation Vida lived with her sister Ollie and family near Choctaw, Oklahoma. Niece Mary Ellen talked of Vida meeting author Louis L'Amour prior to his fame. Mary's version was that he tried getting Vida to go on a date but she refused the invitation. Vida's version was she met him briefly.

In the 1940 US Census Vida states that on 1 Apr 1935 she was living on a farm near Canute in Custer County, Oklahoma. Sometime after that date she left the state of Oklahoma to attended business school in Wichita, Kansas.

Jack Gunter told a story as he'd heard it relating to Vida's enrollment in Business College. He said that one day a traveling salesman showed up at the Gunter ranch selling scholarships into the Kansas educational facility. Telling the salesman he had no money, George Gunter offered to trade an old mule for tuition. The offer was accepted. The salesman left happily with the old mule George figured soon to die. Not long thereafter Vida left for college in Kansas.

In the 1935 US City Directory published for Wichita, Kansas, Vida M Gunter is listed as a student residing at 601 N Volutsia Avenue. In the 1936 edition of the directory she is residing at 415 Fountain Avenue, listing her occupation as a maid.

After completing business school Vida relocated from Kansas to Geary, Oklahoma to live with sisters Hattie and Betty.

By 1940 Vida has left Geary and relocated to Oklahoma City, Oklahoma. In the 1940 US City Directory published for Oklahoma City, Vida M Gunter is listed as residing with sisters Betty and Hattie Miller and their husbands at 222 SE 43rd Street.

In the 1940 US Census taken on April 15 Vida is residing with sisters Hattie and Betty and states she is unemployed and seeking work. Vida reports she is a renter with monthly rental payment being the cost of her expenses. On date of the census Vida states as of March 30 she has been unemployed for thirteen weeks. Census information states she was employed thirteen weeks during the year 1939 and earned a yearly income of $195.00. Vida lists her occupation as Rotumond. (I can find no definition for such occupation.)

In the 1941 US City Directory published for Oklahoma City, Oklahoma, Vida M Gunter is living with her sister Betty and family, residing at 218 SE 43rd Street. Vida lists employment as a clerk at the Federal Reserve Bank.

The 1942 US City Directory published for Oklahoma City, Oklahoma indicates Vida M Gunter has relocated residence to 519 NW 4th Street. She continues employment as a clerk at the Federal Reserve Bank. There is not an Oklahoma City Directory on record for 1943. In the 1944 edition Vida cannot be found listed. The 1945 US City Directory published for Oklahoma City, Oklahoma lists Vida M Gunter residing at her previously given address, 519 NW 4th Street. She continues employment as a clerk at the Federal Reserve Bank.

A story Vida shared with great-niece Robin Dickerson entailing how she met her husband Robert was told as follows: During WW II Vida along with other girls in the area would hop a bus and attend the weekend dance held at Tinker Air Force Base. It was while attending one of the dances she met Bob, her future husband. As Vida stated, "All Bob wanted to do was sit and talk. All I wanted to do was dance. That was what I'd come to do."

The U.S. Department of Veterans Affairs BIRLS Death File, 1850-2010 on ancestry.com has record of Robert F Sanderson enlisting in the US ARMY on 11 May 1942. His release date from service is given as 7 Nov 1945.

Vida Mae Gunter and Robert Frank Sanderson applied for a marriage license in Oklahoma City, Oklahoma County, Oklahoma on 1 Dec 1945. They were married the following day. The marriage license states both were residing at 519 NW 4th Street in Oklahoma City. The couple were united by Harold B Walker, Minister of the First Presbyterian Church in Oklahoma City. Robert (known as Bob) was born on 17 Jul 1918 in Higbee, Missouri, son of Frank Moore and Laura N (Bottoms) Sanderson.

In the 1947 US City Directory published for Oklahoma City, Oklahoma, Vida with husband Robert are residing at 426 NW 25th Street, Apt 11. Robert is listed as 'student' and Vida lists employment as a clerk at the Federal Reserve Bank.

Not long after their marriage, Vida's husband Robert transferred his college education from Methodist University in Oklahoma City to Oklahoma University in Norman, Oklahoma. Following his graduation from OU they moved to Colorado.

In the 1949 and 1951 editions of US City Directory published for Boulder, Colorado, Vida and Robert are residing at 1127 Broadway, Apt F. Robert lists as a student at University of Colorado and Mrs. Vida Sanderson lists employment as clerk at the University of Colorado. While Robert attended Law School Vida worked in the university's business office. On occasion Vida was known to make the remark that she worked to finance her husband through college.

Following Robert's graduation from the University of Colorado they again relocated, this time to Springfield, Colorado. After relocation Vida worked for fourteen years as the office manager for the superintendent of the Springfield School district.

When Robert was elected to the position of District Judge in January of 1966, Vida and Robert relocated to Lamar, Colorado. It was at this time Vida retired and became a full time housewife. In Lamar Robert and Vida purchased a newly built split-level home located at 406 Willow Valley Road. It was there Vida lived out her life.

During his terms as District Judge, Bob and Vida vacationed many places. Some trips were associated with Bob's position, while others were private excursions. Conventions took them across the nation as well as out of country. One vacation they visited Egypt, and on another Australia. They also enjoyed several ocean cruises.

In later years Bob was diagnosed with diabetes. Vida would on occasion mention to niece Mary Ellen the challenge of preparing a meal within the guidelines of Bob's restricted diet. When Vida's mobility deteriorated and Bob had complication arise from the diabetes he was placed into a convalescent center. It was while residing there he passed away.

Judge Robert Frank Sanderson passed away on 1 Sep 2004 in Lamar, Prowers County, Colorado.

With the aid of a part-time housekeeper Vida continued to live in her home and remain socially involved in her community and politics until her death at the age of 95.

Vida Mae Sanderson passed away on 17 Jun 2011 in Lamar, Prowers County, Colorado.

Vida and Robert Sanderson had a private graveside ceremony on 24 Jun 2011 at Fairmount Cemetery in Lamar, Colorado. They also have a dual headstone in the Sanderson family plot at Higbee Cemetery in Higbee, Randolph County, Missouri.

Vida and Robert Sanderson had no children.

The Miller Brothers

Clarence E and **Alvin Oliver Miller** were born 12 Oct 1930 in Geary, Blaine County, Oklahoma to German immigrants, Dr. Emil E and Helena Marie 'Lena' (Albrecht) Miller. Both parents emigrated as young children from Berlin, Germany to the United States in the early 1880s and grew up in Iowa. Before marriage and moving to Oklahoma, Emil Miller completed his dentistry apprenticeship. After he and Lena married, the couple left Iowa to settle in Geary, Oklahoma. Mary Ellen Stevens-Stewart stated that the German language was spoken in the Miller home during Clarence and Alvin's childhood. Dr. and Mrs. Miller had no other children.

Clarence and Alvin were raised in Geary, Oklahoma. They attended Geary School and were both high school graduates.

It is unknown which twin was first born. It was noted when living together Clarence was listed as Head of Household.

Their father, Dr. Emil E Miller passed away in 1928 in Geary, Blaine County, Oklahoma. He was buried at the Geary Cemetery.

Their mother Helena remarried in 1930 in Ardmore, Carter County, Oklahoma to Benjamin Franklin 'Ben' Lowman. They later lived in Tulsa, Tulsa County, Oklahoma. Helena passed away in 1967. She is buried next to her husband Emil in the Miller family plot at Geary Cemetery.

Alvin and Clarence were heavy investors in the stock market. Mary Ellen Stevens-Stewart stated her mother Ollie spoke of the day the stock market crashed, saying it was the first time she'd ever witnessed grown men crying. It was told the brothers took the collapse and their losses extremely hard.

In the 1930 Census Clarence and Alvin are listed as living with their mother at 209 N Arapaho in Geary, Oklahoma. Their mother states she owns the home valued at $5000.00. Clarence and Alvin both give their occupation as trucking, stating they handle all kinds of freight.

Clarence and Alvin each applied for a marriage certificate on 11 October 1930 in Geary, Blaine County, Oklahoma. They married the Gunter sisters on 12 Oct 1930 at the Christian Church in Geary. The wedding date was Clarence and Alvin's 25th birthday.

The next ten years of marriage the Miller brothers and the Gunter-Miller sisters spent living together.

Thanksgiving 1936 a Gunter family holiday gathering was hosted at the home of Betty and Hattie in Geary. Without doing a record search on the property for verification, it is my opinion the residence was the childhood home of Clarence and Alvin.

By the 1940 Census the Miller brothers' mother Helena is living in Tulsa, Tulsa County, Oklahoma with husband Ben Lowman. It is possible she decided to sell the Geary home and this could explain the Miller families' relocation to Oklahoma City prior to 1940.

The 1940 Census states both Alvin and Clarence were unemployed at the time it was taken. The record indicates each had worked 14 weeks during the past year as a pumper for a paving company. It was stated Hattie and Betty had worked 52 weeks during the past year, each working a 48-hour week.

In 1942 Clarence enlisted in the US Army in Tulsa, Oklahoma on 24 August. [viii] It is stated on his enlistment record found on ancestry.com that prior to service his civilian occupation was farm hand/general farm laborer. There is no record found of Alvin registering for the WW II Draft or enlisting in the military. In later years Alvin had difficulty hearing. It is possible he experienced hearing loss at a much younger age thus preventing his enlistment.

In a conversation with Jack Gunter he stated Clarence served during WW II in the Air Force as a tail gunner on a B-17 in North Africa. Clarence supported the Allied Forces in missions during the North African campaigns while a soldier in the USAAF (United States Army Air Force). The North African campaigns ended 13 May 1943, at which time the US II Corps moved into Sicily battling their way on into Italy. The Sicilian/Italian campaigns are where his wife Hattie lost a nephew in action, George Lee Nelson. When Clarence's enlistment ended he was honorably discharged with the rank of Corporal.

Due to his inability to hear, Alvin rarely attended family gatherings in the early 1960s. When guests visited his Oklahoma City home he would excuse himself from the room, leaving Betty to visit with family.

Alvin passed away 6 Aug 1986 in Oklahoma City, Oklahoma County, Oklahoma. His brother Clarence soon followed, passing away on 20 Sep 1986.

The Family in Photos

George and Malisa
Gunter-1930

Malisa w/first grandchild
Julia Nelson May-1916

John Gunter with relative

L-R: Nell, Ollie, Betty, Hattie & Vida Gunter

Bessie and Ollie Gunter

Left Photo:
Betty (R) &
Hattie
Gunter

Right Photo:
John &
Vida Mae
with
mother

Vida Gunter-School Photo

Vida Gunter on her horse Old Alice

George W Gunter

O
L
L
I
E

G
U
N
T
E
R

Betty & Alvin   Hattie and Clarence

George Gunter on Old Alice

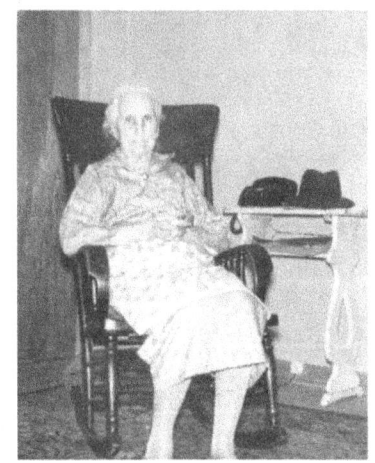

Malisa Gunter

George W. with Sons and Son-in-Laws 1936
L-R Alfred Brown, John Gunter (back), Alvin Miller, George Gunter (Center) Clarence Miller (back), Daniel Stevens (back) Earl Titus and Albert Gunter (taken 1936 Geary Oklahoma)

Gunter Girls--1936
L-R Rosie, Bessie, Ollie, Betty, Nellie, Vida and Hattie

Bessie Brown

Alfred Brown
Nelson
Miller
Miller
Gunter
Gunter
Gunter
Charles Wesley Titus
Nelson
Clarence Miller
Hattie Miller
George Nelson
Gunter
Albert Gunter
Gunter
John Gunter
George Gunter

Elmer Brown
Floyd Brown
Alfred Lee Brown

Janie Gunter
Philotab Gunter
Johnny Ray Gunter
Dorothy Nelson
Jimmy Nelson
Patsy Nelson

Carl Miller
Mary Ellen Stevens
Irene Gunter
Imogene Gunter
A.V. Gunter

Jerry Lee Titus
Nell Titus
Earl Titus

L-R Back Row Rosie Nelson, Robert Nelson, Clarence Miller w/wife Hattie, Ab Gunter w/wife Clara, Ollie Stevens w/husband Dan, Nell Titus w/husband Earl, Margaret Nelson, Bessie Brown
Children Front Row: Patsy Nelson, David Nelson, AV Gunter, Imogene Gunter, Mary Ellen Stevens, Jerry Lee Titus, Dorothy Nelson, Elmer, Floyd and Alfred Lee Brown

Malisa with Children @ 1960 L-R:
Ollie Stevens, Betty Miller, Albert
Gunter, Malisa Gunter, Vida
Sanderson and Bessie Brown

L-R: Hattie Miller, Vida Sanderson, Nell
Titus, Betty Miller, John Gunter, Bessie
Brown, Ollie Stevens, Clarence Miller and
Rosie Nelson

Malisa Gunter with family @1957
Top Row: L-R Ollie Stevens w/grandson Steven Stewart, Nell Titus, John Gunter and Rosie Nelson
Seated L-R Hattie Miller w/Kendal Brown, Malisa Gunter, Betty Miller w/granddaughter Mary Miller, and Bessie
Brown w/great niece Sharalyn Stewart

Gunter Girls
L-R Bessie Brown, Hattie Miller, Betty
Miller, Ollie Stevens, Rosie Nelson and
Vida Sanderson

1963-L-R: Leesa Harrington, Bessie
Brown, Clara Gunter, Ollie Stevens, Betty
Miller w/Itha Harrington and Terry
Harrington

L-R Clarence Miller, Emma and Elmer Brown, Vida Sanderson, Hattie Miller, Carl and Ruth
Miller, Ab Gunter w/Clara, Dan Stevens, Earl and Nell Titus, Betty Miller and Alfred Lee Brown
Front Row: Malisa Gunter, Ollie Stevens, and Bessie Brown (Children pictured are Jerry,
Lonnie and Teresa Brown)

Gunter Grandchildren

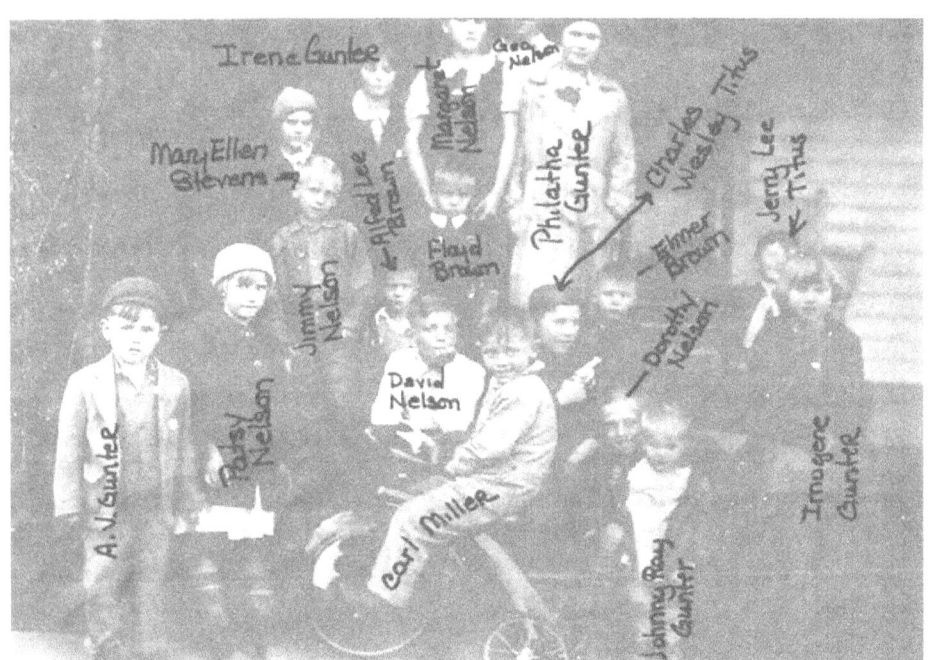

Taken at Gunter family gathering in 1936

A Day at Grandpa & Grandma Gunter's

George Gunter w/grandchildren and Old Alice
Mary Ellen Stevens, Philathia Gunter, and Carl Miller (on horse)

L-R Mary Ellen Stevens, Carl Miller, Elmer Brown, Floyd Brown, Bonnie Gunter, behind her George Wayne
Gunter, Johnny Ray Gunter and Alfred Lee Brown

Family of Albert Gunter

Malisa Jane
'Janie' Gunter

Janie with daughters'
Georgia Lavelle-L &
Sula Loraine

Ruby Gunter w/son
Albert Victor Gunter

Philathia Gunter

Ola Gunter-
Harrington,
daughter of Albert
and Clare Gunter

Philathia with children

Albert V Gunter

Albert V Gunter

John and Imogene
(Jeanne) Gunter

Malisa Jane and
Glenn Harlinger

Clara Peterson-
Gunter

Gerald Gunter and wife Betty

98

Front L-R: Irene, Janie, Philathia, and Imogene
Back L-R: Earline Hill and Gerald G. Gunter

Gerald Gene Gunter

L-R: Tonya and Shawn Gunter, Terry, Leesa & Itha
Harrington, Jeryl Ann Gunter-children of Ola
Gunter Harrington and Gerald Gunter

Left: Stephen Garvin-
grandson of Imogene Gunter

Clara and Albert Gunter w/granddaughter Leesa
Jones/Harrington

Right:
Clara A
Pedersen

Ola Gunter

Ola Gunter

Ola Gunter

Ola Gunter

Ola w/daughter Leesa

Ola w/mother Clara

Above & Right: Ola C Gunter

Ola and Gerald
Gunter

Gerald Gunter
1948

Gerald Gunter

Ola Gunter-Harrington

R: Gerald Gunter

Ola H. and Gerald G. with children: Nicky G (front), Jeryl Ann G (front of Ola), Itha H (center) Terry H (front of Gerald) Shawn G (beside Terry) and Tonya G (front of Terry)

Ola H w/son Terry (L), Itha (far L) Tonya G (front L), Jeryl G (center front) Shawn G (behind Jeryl and ? (R)

Gerald Gunter w/daughters L-R: Shawn, Nicky, Tonya and Jeryl Ann

Tonya Gunter-dau of Gerald Gunter

Gerald Gene Gunter

Gerald and Betty Gunter on wedding day

Nicky Gunter-Barmettler w/ husband James

Shawn and Tonya Gunter, daughters of Gerald Gunter

Daughters of Gerald Gunter
L-R: Jeryl, Shawn, & Tonya

Tonya Gunter
Sr. HS Photo

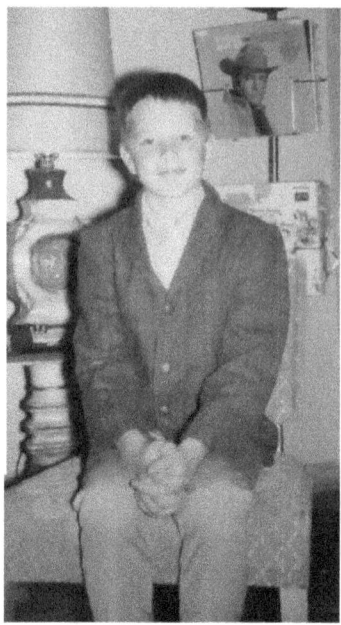

Terry Harrington son of
Ola Gunter-Harrington

Frank Martinez, Jr. (son of
Shawn Gunter-Harrington)
w/wife Jenni and sons
James and Desmond

Frank Martinez, Jr. & wife
Jenni

Upper Photo:
Athena Quilao
& Brad
Kalbfleishch-
Wedding Day

Right: Tonya
Gunter w/ sons
Jake & Garrett
Keen, Lower
Right: Shawn
Gunter-Quilao w/
husband Leonard
and daughters
Veronica and
Athena Quilao

Terry Harrington son of Ola Gunter
Harrington

Terry Harrington

Front L-R: Tonya Gunter, Itha
Harrington, Jeryl Gunter
Back: L-R: Shawn Gunter, Leesa
and Terry Harrington

Jeryl Ann Gunter with children

Leesa Harrington dau
of Ola Gunter-
Harrington

Jeryl Ann Gunter-Harrington

Shawn, Jeryl and Tonya Gunter

Itha Harrington

Johnathan 'Jake'
Keen-Kindergarten
Graduation

Johnathan 'Jake'
Keen-Sr. Graduation
Photo

Krystal Harrington-
Jeryl Ann's
daughter

Frank Martinez, Jr.
son of Shawn
Harrington

Krystal &
Kristopher/children
of Jeryl Harrington

Veronica Quilao

Krystal Harrington

Veronica Quilao

Athena Quilao

Athena Quilao

Veronica Quilao dau of Shawn
Gunter/Harrington-Quilao

Sandra Garvin-Bergthold & unknown

Sandra Garvin-Bergthold-dau of Imogene Gunter

Schuylar Ray Gunter-grandson of John Jr. and Rhonda Gunter,

Garrett Keen s/of Tonya Gunter

Vincent Geesman (grandson of Philathia Gunter-Geesman, great grandson of Albert Gunter) w/daughter Trinity Geesman

GARRETT KEEN

Trinity Geesman w/father Vincent

R-L: Imogene Gunter w/son John Jr. and his wife Rhonda Gunter

Family of Rosa Gunter-Nelson

Robert Perry Nelson

Robert w/sister Gertrude

David Nelson Jr.

Donald Pickett, grandson of Rosa Nelson

George Lee Nelson

David J. Nelson Jr.

Debbie Nelson, daughter of David Nelson, Jr.

Terry Nelson, son of David Nelson, Jr.

Harry Ammerman age 12

Rosa Nelson-1955

On Left: Georgia Nelson, Daughter of George Lee Nelson w/ sister Olivia McBee

Rosa Nelson

Rosa Nelson

Rosa Nelson-1957

Rosa Nelson (Center) w/Dorthy (L) and
Harry Ammerman, Sr. (R) with Harry Jr
and Joe Ammerman

Marguerite Nelson-
Ammerman

Left: Blanche (Patsy)
Nelson-Lutes &
unknown

Harry Sr. and Margaret (Nelson)
Ammerman

Margaret and Harry Ammerman (Center) 50th
Anniversary
Joe and Wanda & Harry Jr and Nancy Ammerman

Thomas and Pat (Blanche Nelson)
Lutes with Margaret (Nelson) and
Harry Ammerman

Front Row: Kenny, Margaret, Aleta, & Harry Jr.
Ammerman
Second Row: Nancy wife of Harry Jr. Kenny's wife, Jeff
and Matt Ammerman

R-L: Harry Ammerman, Sr. , unknown and
unknown, Rosa Nelson, unknown & Margaret
Ammerman

Left: Joe and Wanda Ammerman,
Center Margaret and Harry, Sr. and
Right: Harry Jr. and Nancy Ammerman

Center: Wanda and Larry Ammerman
on their wedding day

Right:

Larry Lee
Ammerman
son of
Wanda and
Larry

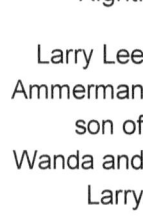

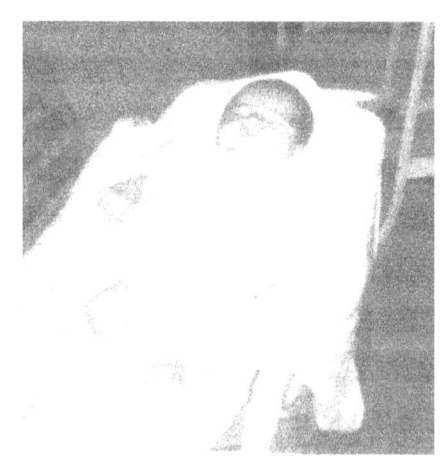

Debbie Nelson dau of David Nelson, Jr.

Debbie Nelson dau of David Nelson Jr.

David Nelson, Jr.

Debbie Nelson w/husband Ted Czernoch

Children of David Nelson, Jr. L-R Debbie, Terry, and Brenda

Upper Left: Wedding of Terry Nelson L-R: David Nelson, Jr. Terry Nelson's wife, Terry Nelson, Marilyn Nelson, wife of David

Upper Center: L-R: Debbie Nelson, Terry Nelson, Brenda Nelson w/Husband Cal Weir

Left: Trisha Czernoch, dau of Debbie Nelson-Czernoch

Right: Jennifer Czernoch w/son and daughter (dau of Debbie Nelson-Czernoch)

Trisha Czernoch-Hylek w/Jeff Hylek

Haley Czernoch-Hylek-age 10

Haley Czernoch-Hylek

Jenna Czernoch-Hylek

Family of Ollie Gunter-Stevens

Ollie Gunter-Stevens with daughter Mary Ellen in 1929

Ollie with daughter Mary Ellen and husband Dan

Ollie with daughter Mary Ellen

Mary Stevens   Age 13

Ollie with daughter Mary Ellen

Mary Ellen Stevens Sr. High School Picture

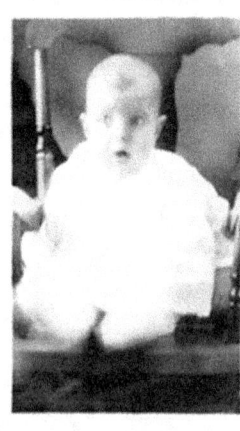

Mary Ellen Stevens

Mary Ellen Stevens 2 yrs. 3 mo.

Mary Ellen High School Graduation May 1947

110

Mary Ellen Age 6

Mary Ellen in HS
Graduation Dress
May 1947

Mary Ellen-Age
10

Mary Ellen

Leonard and Mary-25th Wedding Anniversary

October 1950 Wedding Photo

Mary Ellen Stevens with husband Leonard J.
Stewart

Easter 1960 Leonard and Mary
w/Robin, Sharalyn & Steven

Sharalyn Marie Stewart

Sharalyn Stewart

Sharalyn w/brother
Steven Stewart

Sharalyn Stewart
High
School Graduation
May 1973

Steven Stewart
w/brother Scott

Steven Stewart1st
Birthday-1 Oct 1957

Steven Stewart
Senior Photo 1974

Above: Steven
Stewart-first day
of school 1962

Left: Graduation
from BNC,
Steven on R and
brother Scott

Steven Stewart-2 yrs

Steven Stewart w/dau
Amber

Robin Stewart-1st Birthday 1960

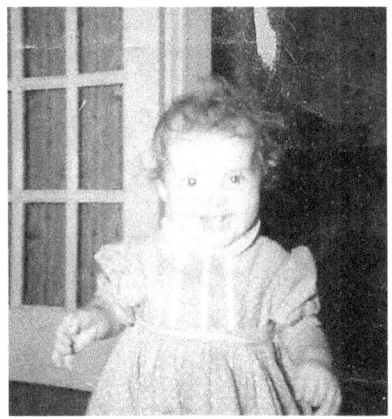

Robin Stewart 1961

Robin during High
School

Mary Ellen w/daughter
Robin Jeanette Stewart

Joe and Robin

Sharalyn , Robin and Steve

Easter Sunday Robin
Stewart

Ollie with
Granddaughter Robin

Robin and Joe Wedding
Photo

Scott Stewart-grade
school photo

Scott Stewart

'Little Scotty'
Kindergarten graduation
2009 son of Scott Stewart

Scotty's children. L-R
Danielle, Sydney, Britni,
and Scotty Stewart

Britni Stewart (L) ,cousin, & Danielle Stewart (R)

Scott and Angela Stewart w/Little
Scotty, Danielle, and Britni

Scott Stewart Family
L-R son Scotty, wife Angela, daughters Danielle, Britni
(holding cousin Lyndee) and Sydney Stewart

KristiLynn Kerbo fishing
Age 4

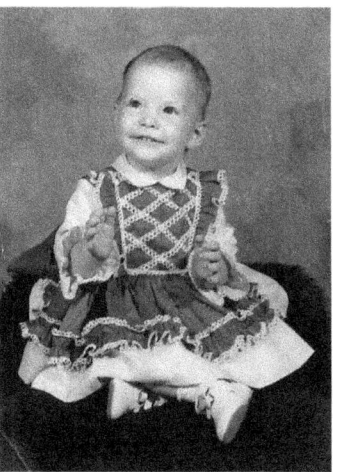

KristiLynn Marie Kerbo

KristiLynn Kerbo's
wedding-May 25. 1997
(dau of Sharalyn Stewart)

Sydney Stewart
Kindergarten
Graduation 2013

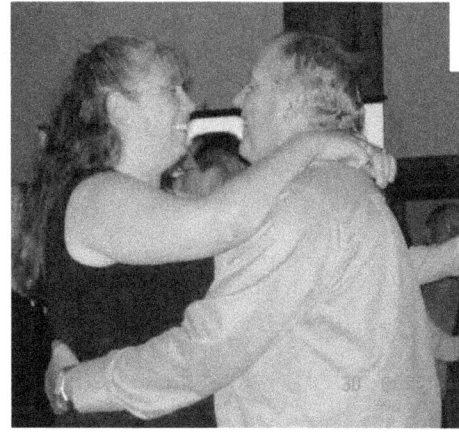

Scott and Angela Stewart

Right: Britni Stewart at Kindergarten
Graduation
Below Right: Steven Stewart (L)
w/granddaughter Lyndee and Scott
Stewart

Amber Leigh
Stewart

Steven Stewart with Daughter
Amber –Aug 2008

Lyndee Fankhauser
granddaughter of Steven
Stewart

Amber, Lyndee, and Tyler
Fankhauser

Lyndee Fankhauser

Christina Dickerson-Stokes
(dau of Robin Stewart-
Dickerson) with husband
Tony Stokes-2012

Mary and Robin Stewart celebrating
July birthdays

Sammy Stokes Easter
2012

Wedding of Amber
Stewart-Fankhauser
Aug 2008

L-R: Scott Stewart,
Steven Stewart,
Amber Stewart-
Fankhauser,
Sharalyn Stewart
and Robin Stewart-
Dickerson

Tripp Stokes son of
Christina Dickerson -
Stokes

Family of Bessie Gunter-Brown

Bessie Gunter-Brown

Brown Boys: Alfred (top) Elmer (L) and Floyd (R)

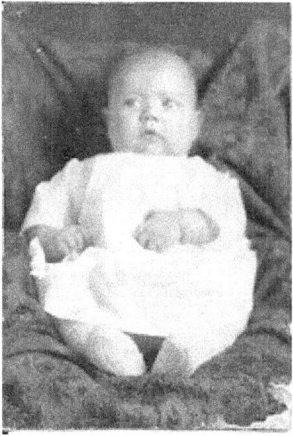

Alfred Lee Brown -3 mo old

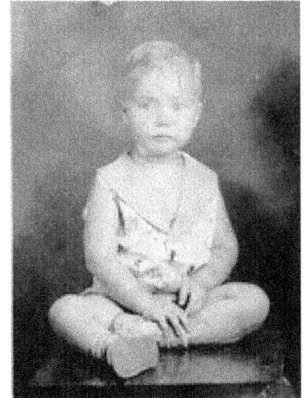

Alfred Lee Brown

Elmer & Emma Brown

Alfred Lee Brown HS Senior Photo

Bessie w/grandson Kendal Brown (R) Robin Stewart, Steven Stewart (L)

Emma Brown with children Jerry Wesley Brown and Sharalyn Stewart

Bessie Brown

Family of John Gunter

John Gunter on Farm Tractor

Johnny Ray and
George Wayne

John Gunter-1975

John Gunter wife Avo holding son Jackie, George (L),
Johnny (R) and daughters Norene, Bonnie and Janet

Johnny Ray Gunter-
1956

L-R George Wayne Gunter, cousin
W.A. Hodo and Johnny Ray Gunter

Johnny Ray Gunter
(L) with Friend

Wedding of Johnny Ray and
Imogene Gunter

Stacy Palmer, LaDonna, Pete
Moulton, Stephanie, Janet, Dick,
Chris, friend, and David Palmer

John Gunter with
grandchildren LaDonna
and Jerry Reed

Jack Gunter

Right:

Bonnie
Ruth
Gunter
w/grand
mother
Malisa
Gunter

Norene (L) and Bonnie

Jackie Gunter

Helen Gunter, youngest dau
of John and Avo Gunter

Jack Gunter w/grandmother Malisa

Helen Gunter

H
E
L
E
N

G
U
N
T
E
R

119

Darlene and George Gunter
w/Family

George Wayne Gunter with
wife Darlene

Darlene and George
Wayne Gunter
2012 Canute Oklahoma

Helen Gunter

Jack Gunter with wife Anne, and
children Conrad and Valerie -
1978

Darlene, wife of George
Gunter with their children

Janet and Norene
Gunter

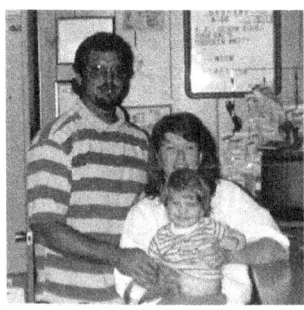

Janet's son Jerry Allen Reed w/wife Lara & son Bradley Allen

David Palmer age 19

Janet w/husband Dick Moulton

Jerry Allen Reed

Janet w/husband K.C. 'Lucky' Palmer

Janet w/1st grandchild, Tasha Maree Adams

David Palmer

Above: Janet with children-LaDonna Elaine Reed, Kelly Palmer (step-dau), Stephanie Palmer, and Stacy Palmer (step-dau)
Left: Janet w/husband Lucky
Left Bottom: LaDonna (dau of Janet) w/husband Rod Bailey and son Alex
Bottom Center: Maigon John Palmer, dau of David Palmer

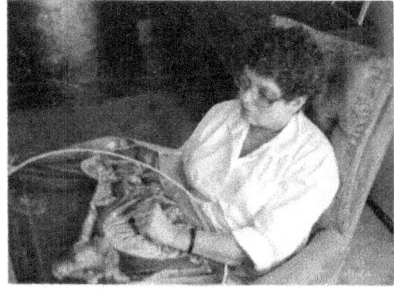

Janet working on a hobby

Janet with sister Bonnie

121

John Gunter w/dau
Norene and her
sons

Norene and Bill Huffman
w/sons Russel, Gary &
David (1978)

Norene and Bill Huffman

Gary Huffman,
age 16

Bonnie Gunter-Rushing

Norene and Bonnie

Bonnie w/son Wade
Trip

Bonnie w/husband Morris Rushing

Family of Betty Gunter-Miller

Betty with son Carl Miller

Carl Miller

Betty with son Carl Miller

Betty Gunter-Miller

Betty Gunter-Miller-1948

Thomas Scott
Hutchison son of Mary
Miller-Hutchison and
David

Betty Gunter-Miller with grandchildren
Mary and Paul Miller

Left: Betty Miller with great-
grandson,
Thomas Scott Hutchison

Carl Miller's Children
Mary and Paul Miller w/pet

Carl Miller

Carl Miller w/friend Pat-1964

L-R: Mary and Paul Miller w/great-
grandmother Malisa Gunter

Family of Hattie Gunter-Miller

Hattie Gunter

Hattie Gunter

Hattie Gunter

Hattie Miller

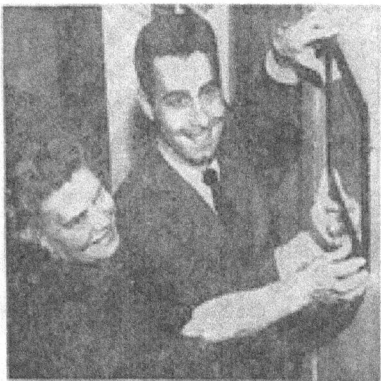

Hattie receiving a
service award from boss

Hattie Gunter-Miller

Hattie and Clarence Miller

Hattie and Clarence's homestead near Colcord OK

Clarence and Hattie Miller

Family of Nellie Gunter-Titus

Christmas Card picturing Nell, Ailene and Earl Titus

Jerry Lee Titus

Ailene Gay Titus

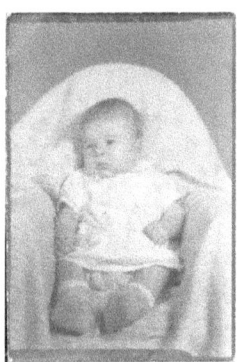

Aileen Gay Titus

Aileen Titus
School Photo-1955

Family of Vida Gunter-Sanderson

Vida Gunter-Age 25

Vida and Robert Sanderson

Vida Sanderson with companions Kelly and Zipper

Vida and Bob on Wedding Day

Robert Frank Sanderson

Judge Robert Sanderson

Vida and Robert Sanderson

Bob and Vida Sanderson

Vida And Bob

Family Reunions

Left: L-R
Betty Miller,
Ollie Stevens,
Bessie Brown,
Avo Gunter
and Bonnie
Ruth Gunter

L-R: Vida, Nell & Ollie
w/Titus Children

L-R: Clarence M., Mary S. , Leonard S., Hattie
M., Ollie S., Nell T. & Bessie B.. Children L-R.
Robin S., Scott S., Sharalyn S., Steven S., and
unknown

Below: L-R Alvin M., Bud H. ,
Clarence M. & Elmer B.

Below Photo Front L-R:
Clarence M, Alvin M, Betty Mw/Leesa H,
Sharalyn S., Robin & Mary S.   Standing
R-L: Hattie M., Ollie S., Rosie N., Ola H.
, Malisa G (behind Alvin)Steven S. ,
Bessie B.

L-R: Ollie w/granddaughter Sharalyn, Betty with
great niece Robin, Helen (front) Bessie, Rosie,
Hattie w/great nephew Steven (front) & Nell

Misc. Photos

Miller Family Gathering
Left: Betty & Alvin w/son Carl, Right: Nickolas Miller, Hattie and Clarence
Miller. Helena Miller (center)   22 Nov 1936

L-R: Ollie Stevens, Carl Miller,
Betty Miller, Vida Gunter &
Betty Jo Miller (best friend of
Mary Ellen Stevens)

L-R: John Gunter, Ollie Stevens, Vida
Sanderson & Hattie Miller

L-R: Hattie Miller, Ollie
Stevens, Vida Sanderson,
John Gunter & Clarence Miller

John, Vida and Ollie

Right: L-R

Leesa w /Itha
Harrington,
Scott, Robin,
& Sharalyn
Stewart, and
Bessie
Brown's
grandchildren

L-R: John Gunter, Ollie Stevens, Vida Sanderson, Hattie and Clarence Miller & Vida's dog Zipper

L-R: Sharalyn, Steven & Robin Stewart w/ dad Leonard

Robert Sanderson, Sharalyn Stewart, and Vida Sanderson   Jan 2004

Vida Gunter with Mary Ellen Stevens

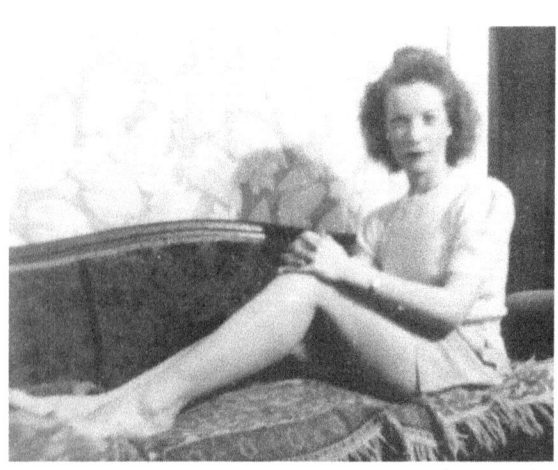

Judge Robert F Sanderson

Above & Right: Vida Gunter during modeling career

Steven Stewart, Malisa Gunter,
Sharalyn Stewart, L-R: Ollie
Stevens, Betty Miller, Bessie Brown,
John Gunter & Rosie Nelson

Hattie & Clarence Miller

Clarence Miller w/ his
organic grown
strawberries

Top L-R: Nell Titus & Betty Miller, Center:
Malisa Gunter, Right: Bessie Brown Children
L-R: ? Brown, Sharalyn Stewart, Kendal
Brown   1960

JUDGES
Aug 18, 1980
Judge Robert F Sanderson (Center)

Swearing Into Office 18 Aug 1980
Judge Robert Sanderson (R)

Appendix

Ruby Willene Stringer-Menard

In an email received 14 Mar 2014, Ruby offers an account of her life as a young girl living on a mountaintop in Arkansas.

The mountain was beautiful. The house was small but comfortable. We had the front room that had a bed and the potbelly stove, and the treadle sewing machine which mama made me some of the most beautiful dresses out of whatever she could find. The cellar was where we stored the potatoes and can goods. Across the road from our front porch was sorghum field.

The kitchen porch looked out over the woods where hogs roamed free behind the fence. Daddy always told me not to ever cross that fence. Well you know this little girl always knew best, so of course you know I had to try. That was the day I found out my daddy was the smartest man in the world. I don't remember what the temptation was but went in the woods. Come to find out it was mating season. The next thing i remember is the biggest black hog on the face of the earth. I do not know who squealed the loudest, me or the hog. Thank God for high top shoes. I was running fast as I could, and could literally feel his breath on my legs. When I jumped the fence his tusk was in the fence below me. Mama saw me from the kitchen.

I remember the mama hogs having their babies in special place daddy had built. We had to get the babies and cut tusk before their mama could get up and oh they could squeal.

I remember daddy and his mules plowing the fields. I don't have any memories off the left side of the house. I remember the stock pin was at the bottom of the mountain. The horses came up in the summer but not the winter. I remember a weeping willow at the bottom because it got used on my legs a few times. I tell everyone I learned the Irish jig very early in life.

We had this fabulous stove in the kitchen where mama kept warm biscuits or corn bread and a big pot of white beans on the back burner and always knew when to put more wood in the door.

I remember daddy got our first car there. It had a rumble seat in it because it closed on me coming down that mountain one time. Mama said I squealed all the way down.

There was a huge oak tree there with a tire swing daddy had hung for me. I saw first a huge black and yellow spider had claimed it for his own. I ran to tell mama she said it was ok it lived in the tree. That swing lost a lot of its magic that day after mama made me kill it if I wanted to swing. Mama told me I had to stand up for what's mine.

Another day I went to gather the eggs. I remembered what mama had said about the spider but that was the biggest snake I ever seen on that nest. I looked at it and decided I needed some advice so I asked mama to pleaseeeeees come tell me how to get my eggs. I was telling her this snake was bigger than me. I found out later she was praying it was not a rattler but turned out to a black snake. She said she would handle it this time because we could not kill it. It was a good snake and you don't kill good things or the bad ones will take over. The rattler came later in the outhouse. Daddy kept a hoe hanged up and mama took care of it but I had night mares about him climbing back up while I was on the little hole."

In an email dated 19 Mar 2014 Ruby stated that during her school years she rode a donkey to and from the schoolhouse.

In another email dated 19 Mar 2014 Ruby shared another story, this one about a motorcycle ride with her husband Alfred.

My husband worked shift work. As I told you, he became a wonderful country boy. He loved to fish and hunt (city style of course). When the kids all got be in school we would stand there waving and wishing them a good day. As soon as they would be out of sight papa ran for the motorcycle and I grabbed saddle bags equipped cast iron skillet and coffee pot, and of course corn meal, lard, and coffee grounds. Off to the river and his favorite fishing hole. Needless to say, we had to go through some wet spots and bogs. This was normal, no issue. This day papa had been shut-up after several days of rain during our fishing time. He was a gluten for punishment. We were so proud of our matching leather sheepskin lined jackets he decided this was our day to shine. We would go to store and get us a cold drink and gas the motor. Just to show off the jackets of course.

We got to the river road and were surprised to see several trucks had gotten there before us. We looked at each other and I stupidly said, "Up to you." I knew what he was going to do so I shouted 'slow and easy'. We did okay for a short ways. Then we came to a dead stop. Water and mud was all the across the road and backed up on both sides. He asked me what I thought. I said it looked a little dangerous to me. The trucks had already been threw it   I had used the wrong word saying 'dangerous'. "Aaaah your tuff," was his response. 'Slow and easy' he forgot. He gunned it, went about six feet in before he went up on the back wheel dumping me back first in the mud hole.

As I was trying to get my feet, I saw him on dry ground laughing at me. Now you know how calm this Irish Indian took this. I told him he'd better give his heart to God for your butt belongs to me. He just kept laughing and I kept slipping and sliding. I finally worked my way out and we went on to the river. I was scheming on revenge but I made happy.

We decided to leave before the trucks. As we got in the middle, I shifted my weight and put my foot down. Down he went, the motorcycle too. My turn to laugh and run. He was not happy.

Author's Notes

--It was stated by Imogene (Jeanne) Gunter that she'd heard her grandfather George W. Gunter had settled the Canute area during the Land Run (Apr 1892). Records point to George and his cousins Ben, Dan, Jonathan 'Cheese', Zack and Wiley Jr. settled near Canute and Foss on remaining unclaimed sections of land during what is sometimes termed 'the Land Rush' which took place in Oklahoma during the late 1890s to early 1900s.

--Ollie Caroline Gunter's birth name may have been Olive as this is the name given on her marriage license. Ollie was often a nickname for Olive.

--In the homestead case file regarding George Gunter's claim there are contradictions. The original claim stated it was filed 12 Feb 1898 and George was of Burns, Oklahoma. The date was later amended to 10 Mar 1898. On 8 Jul 1898 there is yet another amended added to George's land record, changing the property description from Section 20 to Section 17. When 'proving up' on 18 Jul 1904 it was originally stated George had lived and worked on the land for 6-7 years and then was amended to 5 or 6 years. Most land records are specific in date. George testified he established residence on the property 1 Dec 1898. I question this being the actual date he established residence. Where was he living 10 Mar 1898 or 8 Jul 1898? In addition, why wait 5 months to move onto the property? The claimant had six months from date of filing a homestead application to move onto their claim or it was forfeited. They had to live on the land and improve it for a minimum of five years before 'proving up' and had up to seven years after filing claim to prove up or the land was forfeited. A claimant also had the option to cash purchase the 160-acre claim after residing on the claim for 14 months. The cash purchase price was $1.25 per acre.

--The Great Western Cattle Trail often mistakenly referred to as the Chisholm Trail historically followed a path from Texas to near the Canadian border passing through the Canute area and very near, if not alongside the George Gunter homestead. Geographically the Chisholm Trail was 78 miles east of Canute, going through El Reno, Oklahoma.

--During my early years of grade school I said something to my grandma Ollie during one of my visits about her being born in Canute. I presumed it was where she was born since she talked of growing up there. Grandma corrected me stating she was born near Davis, Oklahoma. She then told a story about when she was a little girl they moved to Canute in a covered wagon. After leaving their old home Indians began following them and she remembered watching the Indians from the back of the wagon. If George followed the Ft. Sill/Arbuckle Supply route they would have passed through an Indian Reservation. This may have been a portion of the journey she was making reference to Indians following their wagon for some time before turning back.

-- Mary Ellen Stevens-Stewart has said her grandfather George Gunter had sandy red hair and that she was told his mother had very dark red hair.

--Mary Ellen stated on several occasions that her grandfather, George W Gunter possessed a hunting and fishing card he carried in his wallet. The card allowed him to hunt and fish all year long. She believed he came to acquire the card due to his Indian heritage. Speaking with Native Americans I have not found anyone who knows of such a card ever existing.

--There were a multitude of reasons people came to Oklahoma from Texas between 1880-1900.

1. In 1885 Texas was having a drought. Some pioneer families moved into Indian Territory broke and hoping to start over. In Indian Territory they could rent however much land they wanted for $5.00 a year from an Indian Tribe and secure a lease for 5-7 or 10 years on the land. Everything they raised was theirs to keep. Cattle were plentiful and unbranded wild cattle were free for the rounding up. If they brought cattle into Indian Territory they were taxed 25 cents per head by the Indians. All that was required of a settler by the Indian government was they improve the land by cultivating it and build a home on the rented property. In the area food was plentiful, grass was high, and the soil fertile.

2. Some came to Oklahoma from Texas to assist with building the railroad from Kansas to Texas through Garvin County. Some workers decided to take their wages and lease from the Indians and settle down to farming and/or raising cattle.

3. There were very large cattle ranches in the area always hiring cattle hands. For a wrangler work was plentiful.

4. Many settlers started toward Purcell to participate in the 1889 land run making it as far as Garvin County and stopped there to settle. Some participated in the land run, didn't get what they wanted, and on their way back to Texas settled in Garvin County.

5. Some young men who had cattle experience headed to the area to start cattle ranches where free range was available and cattle could graze all winter without need of feed.

6. Employees working for the government hauling lumber from Texas to Ft. Arbuckle and beyond were drawn to settle in Garvin County.

7. A few were passing through when they secured jobs with merchants, mills, or ranchers to earn a few bucks and decided to settle down.

--Jim Lawson (Malisa Lawson-Gunter's brother) married Effie C Gunter (George Washington Gunter's sister) in Chickasaw Nation Indian Territory a year before George and Malisa married. It may have been how George and Malisa Gunter met.

--The Lawson family may have come to Indian Territory when the Casey family decided to move there. Both families were living in Hood County, Texas in the 1880's. The Lawson's had two daughters (Mary and Elizabeth) who married into the Casey family. Both husbands are buried at Hennepin Cemetery. Mary and Elizabeth are also buried at Hennepin in unmarked graves.

Notes

Index

H

About the Author

Angel and me in Louisiana
2006

I live on an acreage that is a portion of the original farm my parents purchased in 1952, and where grandma Stevens later built a house. It is in that house I have lived the most of my lifetime. I have a passion for animals and have a large furry family consisting of rescues, which share the home place with me.

𝕮𝖎𝖙𝖆𝖙𝖎𝖔𝖓𝖘/𝕰𝖓𝖉 𝕹𝖔𝖙𝖊𝖘

"Texas, Marriages, 1837-1973," index, FamilySearch (https://familysearch.org/pal:/MM9.1.1/F6YS-H3V : accessed 18 Apr 2014), Zachariah Gunter and Sarah A. Hancock, 25 Mar 1882; citing , , reference p 419 rn 22; FHL microfilm 1024887.

Find-A-Grave

Ammerman, Harry Sr	http://findagrave.com/cgi-bin/fg.cgi?page=gr&GRid=19968215
Ammerman, Larry Lee	http://findagrave.com/cgi-bin/fg.cgi?page=gr&GRid=22297149
Ammerman, Marguerite	http://findagrave.com/cgi-bin/fg.cgi?page=gr&GRid=19968207
Bell, Blanche N Nelson	http://findagrave.com/cgi-bin/fg.cgi?page=gr&GRid=15163084
Bell, Raymond Everest	http://findagrave.com/cgi-bin/fg.cgi?page=gr&GRid=34232428
Bergthold, Sandra Garvin	http://findagrave.com/cgi-bin/fg.cgi?page=gr&GRid=81035500
Gunter, Albert Victor	http://findagrave.com/cgi-bin/fg.cgi?page=gr&GRid=27605974
Gunter, Linda Lou	http://findagrave.com/cgi-bin/fg.cgi?page=gr&GRid=27605996
Lawson, David	http://findagrave.com/cgi-bin/fg.cgi?page=gr&GRid=87188477
Lutes, Danny Lee	http://findagrave.com/cgi-bin/fg.cgi?page=gr&GRid=97770434
Miller, Alvin O	http://findagravc.com/cgi-bin/fg.cgi?page=gr&GRid=72934954
Miller, Betty J Gunter	http://findagrave.com/cgi-bin/fg.cgi?page=gr&GRid=72934930
Miller, Clarence E	http://findagrave.com/cgi-bin/fg.cgi?page=gr&GRid=50637032
Miller, Hattie E Gunter	http://findagrave.com/cgi-bin/fg.cgi?page=gr&GRid=50637208
Nelson, David Joel	http://findagrave.com/cgi-bin/fg.cgi?page=gr&GRid=47165830
Nelson, David Joel Jr	http://findagrave.com/cgi-bin/fg.cgi?page=gr&GRid=8250066
Nelson, Ernest James Jr	http://findagrave.com/cgi-bin/fg.cgi?page=gr&GRid=64956638
Nelson, Ernest James Sr	http://findagrave.com/cgi-bin/fg.cgi?page=gr&GRid=93272895

Nelson, George Lee	http://findagrave.com/cgi-bin/fg.cgi?page=pv&GRid=97779613
Nelson, Robert Perry	http://findagrave.com/cgi-bin/fg.cgi?page=gr&GRid=94319008
Nelson, Rosa M Gunter	http://findagrave.com/cgi-bin/fg.cgi?page=gr&GRid=47166204
Nelson, Terry	http://findagrave.com/cgi-bin/fg.cgi?page=gr&GRid=10445254
Osborne, Karen S Lutes	http://findagrave.com/cgi-bin/fg.cgi?page=gr&GRid=8092785
Roper, Philathia B Gunter	http://findagrave.com/cgi-bin/fg.cgi?page=gr&GRid=11237311
Sanderson, Robert F	http://findagrave.com/cgi-bin/fg.cgi?page=gr&GRid=66962302
Sanderson, Vida M Gunter	http://findagrave.com/cgi-bin/fg.cgi?page=gr&GRid=71752787
Snider, Mary Montgomery	http://findagrave.com/cgi-bin/fg.cgi?page=gr&GRid=29582641
Snider, Peter	http://findagrave.com/cgi-bin/fg.cgi?page=gr&GRid=29582665
Snyder, Moses	http://findagrave.com/cgi-bin/fg.cgi?page=gr&GRid=70332438
Snyder, Phoebe Roddy	http://www.findagrave.com/cgi-bin/fg.cgi?page=gr&GRid=70332677
Titus, Evelyn	http://findagrave.com/cgi-bin/fg.cgi?page=gr&GRid=63975019
Titus, Jerry Lee	http://findagrave.com/cgi-bin/fg.cgi?page=gr&GRid=63975020

[i] Ancestry.com. Tennessee State Marriages, 1780-2002 [database on-line]. Provo, UT, USA: Ancestry.com Operations Inc, 2008. Original data: Tennessee State Marriages, 1780-2002. Nashville, TN, USA: Tennessee State Library and Archives. Microfilm.

[ii] http://findagrave.com/cgi-bin/fg.cgi?page=gr&GSln=Snider&GSfn=Moses&GSbyrel=all&GSdyrel=all&GSob=n&GRid=70332438&df=all&

[iii] http://findagrave.com/cgi-bin/fg.cgi?page=gr&GRid=29582665

[iv] http://digital.library.okstate.edu/encyclopedia/entries/C/CA051.html

[v] http://www.legendsofamerica.com/ok-foss.html

[vi] Alvin and Betty Marriage License   https://familysearch.org/pal:/MM9.3.1/TH-1-159393-715124-15?cc=1709399

[vii] Clarence and Hattie Marriage Certificate   https://familysearch.org/pal:/MM9.3.1/TH-1-159393-715122-13?cc=1709399

[viii] Clarence Miller Army Enlistment https://familysearch.org/pal:/MM9.1.1/KMNM-KJY

www.ingramcontent.com/pod-product-compliance
Lightning Source LLC
Chambersburg PA
CBHW080413290526
45791CB00008BA/2252